13

Mike Bartlett's plays include *My Child* (Royal Court Theatre, 2007); *Artefacts* (Bush Theatre/Nabokov/59E59, 2008), which won the Old Vic New Voices Award; *Contractions* (Royal Court Theatre, 2008); *Cock* (Royal Court Theatre, 2009); *Earthquakes in London* (National Theatre, 2010); *Love, Love, Love* (Paines Plough/Theatre Royal Plymouth, 2010). Work for radio includes *Love Contract* and *The Family Man* (both BBC Radio 4, 2007); *Not Talking* (BBC Radio 3, 2006), which won the Writers' Guild Tinniswood Award and Society of Author's Imison Award; *The Steps* and *Liam* (both BBC Radio 4, 2009). He directed D.C. Moore's monologue *Honest* in its first production by the Royal & Derngate Theatre, Northampton, in 2010. He is currently Writer-in-Residence at the National Theatre and Associate Playwright at Paines Plough.

Mike Bartlett

13

B L O O M S B U R Y

LONDON · NEW DELHI · NEW YORK · SYDNEY

Bloomsbury Methuen Drama

An imprint of Bloomsbury Publishing Plc

50 Bedford Square	1385 Broadway
London	New York
WC1B 3DP	NY 10018
UK	USA

www.bloomsbury.com

Bloomsbury is a registered trade mark of Bloomsbury Publishing Plc

First published 2011
Reprinted 2013

Visit www.bloomsbury.com to find out more about our authors and their books
You will find extracts, author interviews, author events and you can sign up for
newsletters to be the first to hear about our latest releases and special offers.

British Library Cataloguing-in-Publication Data
A catalogue record for this book is available from the British Library.

ISBN: PB: 978-1-408-17191-2

Library of Congress Cataloging-in-Publication Data
A catalog record for this book is available from the Library of Congress.

13

13 was first performed in the Olivier Theatre at the National Theatre on 18 October 2011. The cast was as follows:

John	Trystan Gravelle

The Twelve:

Rachel	Kirsty Bushell
Amir	Davood Ghadami
Holly	Lara Rossi
Edith	Helen Ryan
Ruth	Geraldine James
Stephen	Danny Webb
Shannon	Katie Brayben
Zia	Shane Zaza
Mark	Adam James
Sarah	Genevieve O'Reilly
Martin	Nick Blakeley
Rob	Matthew Barker
Alice	Natasha Broomfield
Ruby	Grace Cooper Milton/Jadie-Rose Hobson
Dennis	Nick Sidi
Terry	John Webber
Paul	Nick Blakeley
Esther	Barbara Kirby
Liam	John Webber
Carol	Sioned Jones
Sir Christopher	Martin Chamberlain
Fiona	Zara Tempest-Walters
Sally	Esther McAuley

Other parts played by members of the Company

Director   Thea Sharrock
Designer   Tom Scutt
Lighting Designer   Mark Henderson
Music   Adrian Johnston
Movement Director   Steve Kirkham
Sound Designer   Ian Dickinson

Characters

John

The Twelve:
Amir
Edith
Holly
Mark
Martin
Rachel
Rob
Ruth
Sarah
Shannon
Stephen
Zia

Alice
Carol
Dennis
Esther
Fiona
Liam
Paul
Ruby
Sally
Sir Christopher
Terry

Busker
Heckler
People in the park
Protesters
Riot police
Other police
Passers-by
Various crowds

Other members of the Alpha group

The play should be performed with a circle.

Although the scenes are numbered separately, they should flow continuously.

(/) means the next speech begins at that point.

(–) means the next line interrupts.

(. . .) at the end of a speech means it trails off. On its own it indicates a pressure, expectation or desire to speak.

Act One

One

Darkness.

Laurie Anderson – 'Someone Else's Dream' plays . . . the whole song.

Some light.

We see twelve people asleep in bed.

A little more light . . .

The twelve suddenly wake up.

Amir, Rachel, Holly, Zia, Shannon, Stephen, Ruth, Sarah, Edith, Mark, Martin *and* **Rob.** *All petrified. Disturbed.*

An alarm clock flashing. 7.13am.

John *enters.*

Two

John *is standing with a travelling bag.*

Everyone clears except **Sarah** *who's joined by* **Ruby. Ruby** *drags her own small case, takes her mother's hand.* **Sarah** *checks her emails, they wait for a taxi.* **Ruby** *stares at* **John.**

John *smiles at her. Then looks back out front.* **Ruby** *continues to stare.* **Sarah** *notices.*

Sarah	Ruby . . .
	Ruby . . .
	Ruby!
Ruby	What?
Sarah	Don't stare. (*To* **John.**) I'm sorry.
Ruby	He smells.

Sarah	Ruby! (*To* **John**.) I do apologise.
Ruby	He smells bad.
Sarah	She's isn't normally like this.
Ruby	I am.
Sarah	She's not been sleeping.
Ruby	I have, I'm just precocious. It's you Mom. You never sleep anymore.
Sarah	Ruby! (*To* **John**.) I get bad dreams. I tried to sleep on the plane –
Ruby	Mom?
Sarah	But when I did –
Ruby	Where's Dad?
Sarah	When I did, I . . .

A moment. **Sarah** *stares at* **John**. *He looks at her for the first time.*

Sarah	Oh.

Dennis *enters with the bags.*

Dennis	Hey! Munchkin! What's up?
Ruby	Mum's weird.
Dennis	What?
Sarah	She's being rude again.
Dennis	Come on sweetie! It was a long flight, I know, but we're back home now.
Ruby	This isn't home. This is Britain.
Dennis	You like Britain.
Ruby	No I don't. *Britain?*

She looks at **John**.

Ruby	Britain's ugly.

Three

Ruby, **Dennis** *and* **Sarah** *clear and the stage is charged by a group of protesters and policemen. They clash – shouting. Banners saying 'No fees!', 'We won't pay!'*

Shannon *enters hoovering, listening to her iPod.* **Amir**, *one of the protesters, is arguing with a policeman, both on megaphones. People film it.*

Crowd	We won't pay! We won't pay!
Policeman	Get back!
Amir	We're allowed / to be here!
Policeman	Back! / Now!
Amir	This is a / peaceful protest.
Policeman	Get back!
Amir	I'm not pushing! You're acting / aggressively! This is a –
Policeman	Fuck you –

The policeman pushes **Amir**. **Amir** *pushes back. The tussle continues as . . .*

Four

Ruth *arrives in her office with three advisers –* **Martin**, **Liam** *and* **Carol**. **Shannon** *hoovers.* **Martin** *yawns, loudly.*

Ruth	If you're flagging Martin, I'd get some coffee.
Martin	I'm fine.
Ruth	National insurance and income tax, that's a conversation we haven't had, where's Andrew?
Liam	What?

Ruth	Liam is this skirt working?
Liam	Er . . .
Martin	Andrew's at the conference.
Ruth	I'm sorry?
Carol	The skirt's good, Prime Minister.
Martin	In Brussels!
Carol	It goes with the jacket!
Ruth	What?!
Martin	Brussels!
Carol	Jacket!
Ruth	Excuse me! Do you have to do that now?

Shannon *looks up, leaving the hoover on.*

Shannon	Oh hi! You alright?
Ruth	What?!
Shannon	Well – Not being funny but you look a bit . . .

She does a face.

Ruth	I couldn't sleep.
Shannon	Bad dreams?
Ruth	What?
Shannon	Me too. It's the weather. Makes you sweat like a horse.
Carol	Prime Minister –
Ruth	Look can you do this tomorrow please . . . er . . .
Shannon	Shannon.

Ruth	Sharon
Shannon	Shannon.
Ruth	Just switch it off. Alright?

Shannon, *slightly offended, switches off the hoover. We hear the protest outside.*

Ruth	What is it this morning?
Liam	Student fees.
Ruth	. . . still on that? – Thanks Sharon.
Shannon	Shannon
Ruth	They've started early.
Liam	Haven't we all?
Shannon	I didn't vote for you.

She goes.

Ruth	Can she work here?
Martin	What?
Ruth	If she didn't vote for me.
Martin	As a cleaner, she's technically a civil servant. She can vote for whoever she likes.
Ruth	Carol's a civil servant.
Martin	Yes.
Ruth	Well did Carol vote for me?

*They all look at **Carol**, who's suddenly on the spot. Fortunately for her, **Edith** walks past, grabs a trolley and pushes it through a bank window, then runs off. The police run towards the noise . . .* **Ruth** *despairs.*

Ruth	Martin – Tell them to get that under control. I've got a headache.

Five

The police grab hold of **Rachel**, *who is near the window.*

Rachel   Hey!

Amir   Get off her!

He grabs the trolley and hurls it at a police officer, who falls to the ground. **Amir**'s *then jumped on and arrested. As this happens . . .*

Six

. . . **Stephen** *walks through, to give a lecture to some students at a London university.*

Stephen   At least some of you have bothered to turn
                    up. I'm Stephen Crossley, and today I
                    want to talk about God.

The police charge, scattering the protest, as **John** *walks centre stage. People walking past . . .*

Stephen   I have here a box. Inside is the Lord
                    Almighty himself. You have a choice. Do
                    you open it?

                    If you do, you will look God in the face,
                    and know for certain his existence,
                    dimensions, his absolute power and glory.
                    But unfortunately, once that moment
                    has happened, you will then burn in his
                    omnipotence and omniscience. Your free
                    independent life destroyed, you will be
                    gone forever.

                    Therefore, perhaps you think it's better
                    that you don't open the box. Instead you
                    live a life of horror and worship, always
                    under the power of what might lie inside,
                    waiting for you, in the dark.

So. Do you open it? Do you stare God in
the face? Or shy away.

People in suits, tourists, walk past. **Holly** *on her phone.* **Shannon**
coming home from work.

Stephen   For me. Every time, turn on the lights,
open the box – face the truth. Because
when you do . . .

He opens it. Nothing.

There's nothing there. Never is.

Seven

Alice *enters with* **Mark**. *A* **Busker** *sets up nearby . . . his head is
down, we can't see his face.*

Mark   A toothbrush, a new shirt and a double
espresso. What's his name?

Alice   Mr Hamidi.

Mark   And what's his thing?

Alice   His thing?

Mark   Yeah. What's his –

Alice   I have literally no idea what you're talking
about.

Mark   What's he *done*?

Alice   *I don't know.*

Mark   Alright, look –

Alice   If you mean what's he *accused* of then
maybe I have some –

Mark   Oh for Christ's sake.

Alice	You're a lawyer Mark. What he's *done* is a question for the jury.
Mark	Alice, as you rightly say, I'm a lawyer. What are you?
Alice	I'm good with words. Warwick University, excellent degree.
Mark	2.2
Alice	So I had a good time.
Mark	A toothbrush, a new shirt and a double espresso.

Alice (*giving him the file*)   Assault of a police officer.

Mark	Okay. Give me an hour then burst in, say you need me. Say I've got another meeting, it's an emergency, my brother's ill –
Alice	You don't have a brother.
Mark	Alice, just get me out of there – I'm not at my best
Alice	I'll say. What happened? You're *late*. You're never late.
Mark	. . . the train.
Alice	And your clothes.
Mark	*My* clothes, Alice don't go there, Yellow jumpers, trainers, leggings, you're supposed to be at work.
Alice	That's my thing, my style but you're normally so *fastidious*.
Mark	I had bad dreams okay –
Alice	*Punctilious* – Oh! A nightmare? Wow! Were there monsters?

Mark	Monsters yep. Can we –
Alice	An explosion?
Mark	Yes . . . an explosion . . . monsters – why? Did you have the same thing?

The **Busker** *plays notes on his guitar . . .*

Alice	The same?
Mark	The same *dream*.
Alice	Yes I did!
Mark	That's weird.
Alice	I know.
Mark	Really?
Alice	Yeah.
Mark	*Really?*

Beat. The **Busker**, *pauses for a moment, lifts his head up – a strange expression – deep, depressed . . . then continues . . .*

Alice	No! Course I didn't have the same dream, I don't remember dreams. I spent the night with my boyfriend.
Mark	Lionel.
Alice	Leon. We had lots of sex.
Mark	He's a big chap right?
Alice	Absolutely he's a big chap yes.
Mark	I meant fat.
Alice	I meant his cock.
Mark	You're odd.
Alice	I'm alternative.
Mark	Get my things.

Alice   Go to your meeting.

Mark   What's his name again?

Alice   Amir Hamidi.

Alice *goes.* **Mark** *has a searing headache. He leaves, just as . . .*

Eight

. . . **Rachel** *enters on the phone.*

Rachel   Amir Hamidi. Amir. Hamidi, he's been
                     arrested, no I don't want to hold I've been
                     holding already don't you dare fucking
                     put me on hold okay if you transfer me
                     or move me or do anything with me I'll
                     scream I'll call you back and just scream
                     down the phone or something – all I want
                     to know is where he is and you're going to
                     find out and tell me now yes? Now. That's
                     what you're going to do. So.

                     Hello? Hello?!

They've hung up. She screams, throws her phone away in anger –
John *catches it.*

John   Rachel?

The busker stops playing. **Rachel** *looks at* **John**.

Rachel   Oh God.

                     God . . .

                     John? How can . . .

She looks at him. Hits him.

                     We thought you were dead.

She hugs him. Tight.

Nine

A meeting in Number 10. **Ruth** *and* **Dennis** *shake hands.*

Ruth	Mr Harrison. Your reputation precedes you.
Dennis	Thank you Prime Minister. Please call me Dennis.
Ruth	Did you have any trouble getting here, through the crowd?
Dennis	No, they threw some eggs but –
Ruth	Well you can't make an omelette.

A tiny beat.

Dennis	I'm sorry?
Ruth	It's an expression – you can't make an omelette without –
Dennis	I can –
Ruth	Okay –
Dennis	I can make an omelette, I'm pretty good –
Ruth	What?
Dennis	Two eggs, cheese, mushrooms.
Ruth	Ah. You're joking.
Dennis	Yeah.
Ruth	Ha ha.
Dennis	Thought I'd break the ice.
Ruth	This isn't official is it? This visit?
Dennis	No Prime Minister. If it were official you'd be talking to the Ambassador. The President felt perhaps if the two of us

were to speak instead it would be more . . . informal.

Ruth   Well he's right so far. I'm told you have the President's ear. Apparently you go way back.

Dennis   Way back yeah.

Ruth   The President's an interesting man, Dennis. I thought we were getting on and there was mutual respect, but recently – nothing. Suddenly there's silence. And that's not on.

Dennis   He's a busy man. That's the Ambassador's message.

Ruth   I know that's the Ambassador's message but no one likes the Ambassador, no one tells him anything. I assume the President sent you informally like this because he knows I've had enough of the *message* and at last you're going to give me a *reason*.

She smiles. **Dennis** *likes her.*

Dennis   It's Iran. The talks. The President hopes the Iranians will believe there is distance between our two countries. He doesn't want it to seem like we're secretly building a coalition to invade.

Ruth   We're not.

Dennis   Not yet. Right now he's still in the 'extending the hand of peace' stage. He's talking about new global alliances. But if that fails the old alliances will be as important as ever. So what I'm saying is, you're right, there is silence, but you can read something into it.

Ruth	
Dennis	The silence contains an implicit friendship. He can't articulate that friendship or it would defeat the point.
Ruth	That's why you're here.
Dennis	That's right.
Ruth	You're asking for patience.
Dennis	Yes.
Ruth	Faith.
Dennis	Exactly. Yes. Yes Prime Minister. Have faith.
Ruth	
Dennis	When the talks are over, it'll be the specialist relationship we've ever had. Press opportunities, private conversations. Whatever you need, you get, but at the moment things between Britain and America have to seem . . . cold.
	The talks are working. We stand a chance of averting the inevitable. And that's rare. No one wants a war.

Beat. **Ruth** *smiles.*

Ruth	Alright. Tell the President he has my support.
Dennis	Thank you.
Ruth	For now.
Dennis	Understood.
Ruth	And you'll keep me updated.
Dennis	Yes we'll make sure we –

| **Ruth** | No. You. Dennis. You're the President's man, I think you know what's going on better than anyone, so you'll keep me updated, you'll be on the phone all the time, here when I need you, as long as this goes on. That's the price for my patience. Okay? |

Dennis *smiles.*

| **Dennis** | Okay. |
| **Ruth** | Good. Martin will show you out. |

Dennis *goes.*

Ten

. . . **Rachel** *walks in front of* **John**, *angry.*

Rachel	He's been arrested, we were out protesting and got into a fight and they took him off. I don't know where he is. And you know, then you're just . . . standing there looking like a fucking – How did you know I'd be here?
John	I didn't.
Rachel	Where did you go? Why did you leave us? Don't *smile* don't – We have things to deal with John big fucking things hanging in the air the air is thick right now with this – don't think we're friends –
John	It's good to see you.
Rachel	I'd forgotten but it's coming back quickly how annoying you can be.
John	You and Amir. Still together.
Rachel	Yeah we are. Still together. Yeah.

Beat. She looks at him – so?

John	What are you up to?
Rachel	Huh! Okay – Yeah John– let's catch up, lets sit down and have a proper good old chat about how things were and where we are now and what's gone on. So I'll start – Amir was working as a lecturer which was nice but then they lost funding, shut the department so now he's miserable as fuck and as for me, well, I was doing my PhD but gave it up cos one of us had to earn something. So now I have a job. I work for a charity. Women's rights in developing countries.
John	Your sort of thing.
Rachel	I sit on the phone and call people up and ask them for money.
John	Like sales.
Rachel	It's begging. So! What about you John? What have you been *up to recently*?

Beat.

John	Things are difficult.
Rachel	That's perceptive of you yes difficult is a word that's a good word to describe it literally every day I get a call, an email, this person's ill, that one's depressed, I'm a walking Samaritan people think I can deal with their problems but for some reason they never imagine I might have some of my own cos I'm not sleeping at the moment.
John	Bad dreams?

| **Rachel** | No not bad, horrific, if you want the truth, which I remember you always did – so why did you go then? Leave us. How could you? No one understood it. |

A beat.

| **John** | There's a Starbucks over there. I need to wash. I'll sort myself out, come back in a minute? Alright? |

She looks at him.

| **Rachel** | You'll come back? |

He smiles and turns to go.

| **Rachel** | John? |

He looks at her.

I'm glad you're not dead.

Eleven

Amir *is sat at a table.* **Mark** *walks in.*

Mark	I'm Mark, your solicitor.
Amir	You?
Mark	Yeah.
Amir	I've changed my mind. I'm pleading guilty.
Mark	Look, I don't want to be here either mate, but you phoned your girlfriend, she called your dad, he checked the Yellow Pages, and here I am, under-paid, over-qualified, you might as well use me. I'm really good.
Amir	You're a wanker mate.

Mark	What's the charge?
Amir	Those papers, doesn't it say?
Mark	Can I make a confession?
Amir	Okay.
Mark	I haven't read the papers.
Amir	Fuck's sake.
Mark	I *know*. I haven't read them. What a *dick*. So. The charge.
Amir	I was protesting, and this police officer was kicking my girlfriend so I got this trolley and sort of pushed it at them. One of them goes down and I'm like shit. We weren't being violent, it was them, one of them calls me Al-Qaeda, he's swearing all of that, and I'm trying to stay out of it but –
Mark	What were you protesting against?
Amir	Student fees.
Mark	Aren't you a bit old for that?
Amir	I was a lecturer. I got fired.
Mark	Well you should be all in favour then. Bit more money in the system you can keep your job.

Over the next speech, **Mark**'s *nose slowly starts bleeding.*

	I had a great time at university. Parents paid for it of course. And I got in just before they started charging so *ker-ching*. What do you want instead then? What's your alternative?
Amir	A graduate tax would be more / successful in –

13

Mark	Yeah but that's the same thing. You pay as tax, you pay off a loan, doesn't make any difference. Either you want properly funded universities or you don't. It's a competitive world these days. India. China. We're on the way down.
Amir	Oh – you've got –
Mark	I just think it's funny that essentially you're protesting because they *called it the wrong thing*. You got into a *fight* – I thought you must really mean this stuff but no, you're just unemployed and pissed off. Anyway. We can get you out of it, if you say the right things.
Amir	Your nose is bleeding.
Mark	What?
Amir	There's a whole load of blood coming out of your nose.

Mark *smiles, then puts his hand to his nose.*

Mark	Shit . . .
Amir	Is it stress?
Mark	What?
Amir	Or coke?
Mark	No.
Amir	
Mark	. . .
Amir	You want to go and sort yourself out.

Twelve

Thirteen members of an Alpha course enter and sit in a semi-circle.
*Holly's with them but a bit mistrustful. **Sally** is the leader.*

Sally	So in this half, I thought I might ask a few questions of those who have contributed a little less so far. Holly! Maybe you could tell us what brought you here and what you hope to get out of these sessions?
Holly	Er yeah. So I want something good to happen? Cos my dad's a shit, and my mum gets anxious, about things? And I'm not liking university cos I haven't got any money or . . . well, friends. I don't know why, I'm a good person I think but anyway my gran, she goes to this church and I was telling her and she said I should try the Alpha course cos you only work out what you want to do in life when you know what your core beliefs are so . . .
Sally	Alright. Terry – perhaps the same question to you.
Terry	Well, I suppose it was my ex-girlfriend who first –
Holly	Okay wait you ask me this big question then we move on? I thought we were here to talk?
Sally	We are, and it was important to hear that Holly but –
Holly	I was opening up. I was answering.
Sally	And I appreciate that but –
Paul	You know sometimes the questions are more important than the answers.

Holly	What?
Paul	Sometimes the *questions* are more important than the *answers*.
Holly	What does that mean?
Sally	It's a very good point and worth considering, for all of us. Maybe real belief isn't about facts, certainties, *answers*. It's questions, possibilities. Who are we? What are we doing here?
Holly	I'm definitely starting to ask what I'm doing here.
Sally	Terry do carry on.
Terry	My ex-girlfriend had this dress and –
Holly	But it is about certainties. It all is.
Sally	Holly –
Holly	There's one God, original sin, Jesus, the Trinity, heaven, hell. Those aren't questions, they're given as facts.
Sally	You sound very familiar with Christianity –
Holly	My dad was a priest.
Sally	I thought you said your dad was a shit.
Holly	Bible in one hand, bottle in the other.

They're all quiet for a moment, intimidated, **Holly** *presses on . . .*

> I have trouble believing in any of it. Why would God let me be born into a fucked up family with no money and a shit life when I've done nothing, absolutely *nothing,* to deserve it?

A moment.

Esther	Can I say something?

Sally	Esther – of course.
Esther	It seems to me Holly. Holly, is that your name?
Holly	Been here all afternoon *Esther* –
Esther	It seems to me that God allows us freedom to make *our own* decisions. Yes? If you're having difficulty and torment in your life maybe that's more about your *attitude*? Your *approach*.
Paul	But, to be fair to Holly, it's a big question that every Christian struggles with. If there's an all-powerful, all-loving God, why is there evil in the world?
Esther	And that's what we're here for, to ask those big questions.
Sally	Yes, Esther, that's right exactly.
Holly	So what's the answer?
Beat.	
Esther	Well . . .
Holly	Yeah and here's another big question – Why did the Jesus turn up then? Right then? He could've freed the African slaves, or stopped Hitler killing the Jews, but no, he came to Earth at that point and did a few small miracles. He could actually come down right now, do some miracles today, help us all out with the climate, money, terrorism, we could do with that but I don't see him anywhere.
Paul	Well, Jesus never claimed to *solve* / our problems.

Sally	So you're basically saying you don't believe in God.
Holly	What?
Sally	That's what your questions imply.
Paul	Er . . . Sally, I don't think that is what she –
Sally	That's what *all* your questions imply.
Paul	Maybe we should / take another break?
Sally	This is a Christian group, a Christian discussion group –
Holly	I know. It's a discussion group and we're / discussing it.
Sally	I'm in charge of how it runs and I want to make it constructive, and open but you're just – You're just sat there and –

She starts crying. **Paul** *comforts her.*

Paul	It's alright. Hey . . . Hey . . .
Sally	Sorry but she's . . . I know she probably doesn't understand, but she's horrible – Terry. It's your turn. I want to hear from Terry.
	Terry! Say something! Please!

A pause. **Terry** *isn't sure. The pressure is huge.*

Terry	Sometimes I hear voices.

They all look at him. A moment.

Holly	Wow.

Esther *turns to* **Holly***, sweetly.*

Esther	Holly?
	Look . . .
	Maybe you should just fuck off?

Holly *grabs her bag and goes.* **Edith** *starts practising the piano.*

Thirteen

Ruth *is making a speech.*

Ruth   It's tough for everyone at the moment so
I think some plain speaking is called for.
I'm not an old Etonian, I'm not one of
the boys. My father was a postman, my
mother a primary school teacher. I've
come a long way, and I'm proud. Under
my leadership, the Conservative Party
has modernised, root and branch. Just as
Labour grew up from outdated socialism,
so we have moved on from the days of
Thatcher. We get, now, the importance
of the NHS, of comprehensive schools,
of a state which looks after people. We
don't hold up the *market* as a solution to
everything, but unlike many currently
in opposition, we're also not frightened
of it. We stand for opportunity. We want
people to get on and I promise you we'll
get this economy back on track – this time
through hard work, not gambling and
speculation. This time through enterprise
and getting out there and getting it done.
That's what I'm all about. Nothing was
ever handed to me on a plate. I like hard
work. Every minute. Every hour. To make
this country great again. That's what you
voted for. That's what you're going to get.
Okay? Hard work!

She smiles. Cheering as . . .

Fourteen

. . . **Ruby** *runs on and sits at a table.* **Sarah** *brings dinner over
and she eats.*

Ruby   I prefer it when Amelia cooks.

Sarah	You're so lucky Ruby
Ruby	I know.
Sarah	Most children don't have a cook.
Ruby	I know but I do have a cook and I prefer her food to yours.
Sarah	Some children don't even have a mommy.
Ruby	What does that mean? Is that a threat?
Sarah	No. A threat? Of course it's not a threat.
Ruby	You have food you like and don't like. The cook's a professional, you're not. It makes sense that I prefer her food. I'm allowed to express my opinion.
Sarah	I'm saying you should be grateful.
Ruby	To who?
Sarah	That you have food and shelter at all.
Ruby	*Thanks Mom.*
Sarah	Not to me Ruby, not to us, grateful you were born into such a well-off background in the first place.
Ruby	You mean grateful to God.
Sarah	Yes, absolutely. Grateful to God.
Ruby	I don't believe in God.
Sarah	I beg your pardon?
Ruby	When you say grace, I don't shut my eyes, I just wait for you to stop.

Beat.

Sarah	Ruby, you should be careful.
Ruby	What do you mean?

Sarah	It's.
	It's
	It's all a matter of responsibility is what I'm saying sweetheart, beliefs come with responsibilities. You can't just sit there and say something like that, something like 'I don't believe in God' you have to have a philosophical basis for it, you have to be able to justify it.
Ruby	I can believe what I like.
Sarah	Where do you get this from? It's not me certainly, it's not your father.
Ruby	I read a book.
Sarah	When you open your mouth and these things come out – it's not the Ruby I like.
Ruby	I appreciate a multiplicity of voices in my life rather than simply relying on my parents.
Sarah	What book?
Ruby	I read lots of books.
Sarah	*What book?*
Ruby	*Fairytale God* by Dr Stephen Crossley.

Pause.

Sarah	I would really appreciate it, Ruby, if as a favour to me, you ate your chicken.

Ruby *reluctantly does.*

Ruby	You were shouting last night.
Sarah	What?

Ruby	You were shouting in your sleep. God. God! Help me. Save us! Save us!
Sarah	It was a bad dream.
Ruby	That's what religion is.
Sarah	What *are* you?
Ruby	Just a *bad dream*.

Fifteen

Amir *walks with* **Rachel** *from the interview room.*

Rachel	He said it was a coincidence.
Amir	I don't believe in coincidence.
Rachel	Neither do I but there he was.
Amir	Didn't you say like what the fuck?
Rachel	Of course but he wouldn't tell me. He asked about these dreams – anyway then when we found out where you were and when we got here, he marched straight up to the desk and I don't know what he said but after a couple minutes they let you out – I mean actually of all people he was the one we needed but –
Amir	Is he alright?
Rachel	What do you mean?
Amir	He's not ill, or –
Rachel	No he's not ill, he's just the same, he's . . . John.

They've arrived at **John**. **Amir** *looks at him.*

John *looks at* **Amir**. *Smiles.*

| **John** | You're okay? |

Amir	Yeah.
John	You look good.
Amir	Thanks.

Mark *enters with a tissue.*

Mark	I go to the bathroom to sort myself out, when I come back they tell me you've been let off. What happened?
Amir	John got me out.
Mark	John? Okay. This is John. And he's what? A friend? A wizard?
John	I asked them if they were going to press charges.
Mark	They hadn't pressed charges?
John	Did you check?
Mark	Well, I assumed since his daddy was willing to pay –
John	They didn't have any evidence. It's good. He's out. What's the problem?

Mark *looks at them.*

Mark	Nothing.
John	You wanted to help him.
Mark	Help him? No. Sorry. Heart of stone. I'm very happy he's out of my life. Fucking over the. . . you know . . .
Amir	Moon?
Mark	*Rainbow.* Seriously. Can do without it.
John	Is that a latte?
Mark	Cappuccino.

| **John** | I haven't had a cappuccino in ages. Do you mind? |

He takes it and drinks.

	You look tired.
Mark	Don't look so great yourself –
John	Bad dreams?
Mark	I'm *sorry*?
John	Monsters. Darkness. What did you say Rachel? Something moving? An explosion? What's your name?
Mark	Mark
John	Mark.

John *gives the coffee back.*

| | How did you sleep last night? |

Mark *takes the coffee – looks at* **John**. *Unsure for a second.*

| **Mark** | Have you been talking to Alice? |
| **John** | Who's Alice? |

Alice *enters, out of breath.* **Mark** *looks straight at* **John**.

| **Alice** | Oh! Mark! There you are! You've got to come right now because something really terrible has happened to your . . . er . . . brother . . . he's really . . . dead . . . what? |
| **Mark** | Come on. |

Mark *leaves.* **Alice** *follows.* **Rachel** *and* **Amir** *look at* **John**. *He smiles.*

| **Amir** | You're alright? |
| **John** | Yes. |

Amir	Cos we thought since you never called us or told us anything, we assumed there must be something wrong with you.
John	
Amir	
Rachel	You know what we did?
Amir	Rach, give it a minute – let's find somewhere to –
Rachel	No I'm going to tell him right now actually – the morning you'd first gone no one knew anything but we assumed you'd turn up but then there was another day and the next day and course the assumption was that eventually you'd come back but once it was months and then years it was like, how long do we keep on waiting?
John	I'm sorry if it was / difficult.
Rachel	Too late. So in the end we had a funeral. Me, him, and whatever other people remembered who you were and cared which by then it wasn't many if we're honest but we got together and said goodbye cos we thought he has to be dead because if he *isn't* dead then we don't know him at all. Doing that to us. So we said goodbye and we buried you, didn't we?
Amir	Yeah.

A beat.

John	Do you want to come out? Tonight. I haven't been out in a long time.

Rachel	No, of course we don't want to come *out*. John –
Amir	It's been a long day.
John	Of course. I'll see you later then. Is it alright to stay with you?
Rachel	For how long? I don't see why –
Amir	Yeah, it's okay.
John	Thank you.

He turns to go.

Rachel	What are you going to do? Do you even have any money?
John	I'm fine.
Rachel	You want to borrow some?
John	No. I'll be fine. Thanks though.

And he's gone.

Sixteen

Holly *is with* **Edith**. **Edith** *is giving her some money.*

Edith	How much do you need? Thirty?
	There. Have a nice time. Just this once.
Holly	Thanks Gran.
Edith	Yes. Go for your life. No regrets. You're young.
Holly	Yeah.
Edith	You've always got to remember in life, the most important thing . . . The most important thing you'll ever learn . . .

Holly	What?
Edith	. . .
	Oh! Look at you. Holly! Dressed up. Lovely. You're going out tonight?
Holly	Yeah.
Edith	Are you alright for money?
Holly	No . . . Gran . . . it's . . .
Edith	How much do you need love?

Holly *looks at* **Edith**.

Holly	Thirty?
Edith	Alright.
	There. Just this once. Have a nice time.

She goes into her handbag, gives her thirty quid, **Holly** *takes it, and goes.* **Edith** *plays on the piano and it becomes music under the next scene.*

Seventeen

Ruth *is having a drink with* **Stephen**.

Stephen	I don't mind admitting, I was surprised. You told me you've started praying again, so I just assumed this would be it. But I listened to every word and once again, no God.
Ruth	People don't want to hear what I believe, it's about what I think.
Stephen	People want you to be honest.
Ruth	About my judgement, my views on the world.
Stephen	And your belief in God informs that of course it does, and if your belief informs

your decisions it's dishonest not to mention it in a speech on standards, it's actually anti-democratic.

Ruth This was supposed to be a relaxing evening for me. One night off in two months, I think what shall I do? I know, I'll get Stephen round, he's a laugh.

Stephen Ignore me Ruth – keep doing whatever you're doing because you're loved. The masses trust you, and vox popull vox dei.

Ruth You think Latin's sexy don't you?

Stephen Latin's wise. Greek is sexy. I can explain your success Ruth. You are your work. You're a woman of the people, for the people. I mean it's a strain for you from minute to minute I'm sure, but your greatest strength?

Ruth Enlighten me.

Stephen No husband. No children.

Ruth Thank God my son is dead and my husband left me, how lucky am I?

Stephen You've got nothing to fight for except your country. It's like you're a priest. No commitments, distractions, you're married to us. People like that. Thatcher was the same.

Ruth Thatcher had kids.

Stephen But she didn't give a shit about them. The public think men are better at detachment. Separating their work decisions from their home life.

Ruth That's rubbish.

Stephen Well you don't have a home life.

Ruth	I do, I get in, I put the television on.
Stephen	Friends?
Ruth	Never seen it.
Stephen	*Do you have any friends?*
Ruth	Of course.
Stephen	Who?
Ruth	You're a friend.
Stephen	Who else?
Ruth	. . . Oh Stephen I don't have time.
Stephen	Don't worry. You'll manage with the two of us. Me and Uncle Pinot. We'll be there for support when you need it.

He tops up her wine.

	And you will. In the next few months you're going to need all the support you can get.
Ruth	I've got support. You said, I'm popular –
Stephen	Personally. You're going to need solid personal back up when you're sending other people's children to their death.

Beat.

Ruth	Let's talk about something else. How's your sex life?
Stephen	My sex life?
Ruth	Or something, *anything,* I don't know!
Stephen	Currently my sex life is tepid. How's yours?
Ruth	Like a mammoth.
Stephen	Woolly?

Ruth	Extinct.
Stephen	Must be tricky for a woman like you.
Ruth	Sometimes I get so horny I have to go for a walk.

The music changes to a club beat – throbbing noise . . .

Stephen	What's this?
Ruth	I don't know. Radio must've retuned itself. It's one of these digital ones, sometimes it just does its own thing.
Stephen	You still dance?
Ruth	What? No.
Stephen	I remember as a student you dancing so hard you knocked the rector's teeth out.
Ruth	He got in my way.
	No. After Simon died, I never saw the point.

The music and momentum builds . . . builds . . .

I'm not sleeping at the moment Stephen. That's the problem.

Every night, this dream . . .

Eighteen

People are dancing – the people of London, out on the town – drunk and letting go. It's tribal and free and open. Full-hearted shouting and release. The student party after the protest maybe, or a dream, a memory . . . It builds and builds and then . . . with a ripping . . . voice and voices . . . the world explodes . . . white light – a nuclear blast and then . . .

Blackout.

Act Two

One

The same music as before: Laurie Anderson – 'Someone Else's Dream'.

Then it's cut short –

The twelve awake in bed, as before. Terrified. Breathing. A terrible vision.

Bright light – the alarm going – 7.13am.

Two

*Everyone clears except **John** reading on an iPad, **Mark** making coffee and **Ruth** with a cup of coffee. **Carol** reads from a paper, bored, annoyed . . .*

Carol	The thirteen steps is . . . a paragraph of the Final Document of the 2000 review Conference of the Nuclear Non-Proliferation Treaty. It provides a set of . . . 'practical steps for the systematic and progressive efforts to implement Article VI', which is the part of the –

A big sigh.

	– Treaty that provides for nuclear disarmament. So . . . that's what you need to know when it comes to Iran. The thirteen steps are the proof that we've . . . er . . . made an effort.
Ruth	What's the matter Carol?
Carol	It's rather early.
Ruth	Well no rest for the wicked.

| **Carol** | I wouldn't know. |

Beat.

Ruth	What are they? Specifically. The thirteen steps.
Carol	You want all of them?
Ruth	Of course. Is it long?
Carol	Well there's thirteen of them.
Ruth	We'll do it in the car.
Carol	The Foreign Secretary's in the car. You asked to see him this morning?
Ruth	Alright. Good. Bring my coffee. We'll test him.

She goes with her BlackBerry. **Carol** *picks up her coffee and follows.*

Three

John *is in* **Amir** *and* **Rachel**'s *flat.* **Amir** *hasn't slept – he's slightly wild, fidgeting, restless . . .*

Amir	I don't want to sleep. I stay up, putting it off, but eventually you do and there's figures in the dark, this *feeling*, something horrific – thousands of voices, insects. And I'm there with Rachel, in the dream and something terrible's about to happen, there's an explosion and then we wake up, facing each other, screaming. Every night.
John	I'm sorry.
Amir	How can it be both of us? Exactly the same thing? Do you get them?
John	No.

He looks at **Amir**.

John	What are you doing today?
Amir	I've got some job applications I'm supposed to fill in, and eventually I have to sign on . . . I don't know . . .

He sits on the sofa.

Yesterday was this big moment, we all went out, an early start, we were like 'get it back on the agenda, in the headlines' – but then you get there and the turns out's not as many as you think, the police are aggressive and then everything that happened and you come home and you just *know* you haven't made any difference at all. They just sit up there in that fucking building and they really – I really don't think they give a shit.

He switches on his laptop.

John	I thought you were going out?
Amir *shrugs.*	
John	I need a box.
Amir	What kind of a box? A cardboard box?
John	Probably needs to be wood. It might rain. I suppose no one has wooden boxes anymore do they?
Amir	What for? We've got a bucket?
John	That'll do.
Amir	Under the sink. Why? What are you doing?
John	I'm going to the park.
Amir	Why?

| **John** | You should come along. |

| **Amir** | What are you doing? |

John *looks at him.*

Holly *walks towards* **Mark**'s *breakfast table, wearing a dressing gown with hood up.*

| **John** | Come with me. |

Amir *looks at him for a second –*

Then –

| **Amir** | Nah. I'm tired. I'll just stay here. |

John *looks at him and goes.*

Four

Mark *comes up to the breakfast table.*

| **Mark** | Thank God you're alive, I thought I might've actually fucked you to death. Good way to go. As long as you orgasm first. Can you imagine having a heart attack before you come? Coffee? |

Holly *takes off her hood.*

| **Mark** | Jesus. Some girls look great first thing, no make-up, fuzzy hair, some girls look really sexy in the morning. But you? You're . . . feral. There. |

He gives her the coffee.

| **Holly** | I didn't mean to sleep over – but it was late . . . |

| **Mark** | It's fine. Like having a girlfriend. I was up at four. Bad dream, explosion, monsters, all kinds of shit, I went to the living room and binged on *CSI: Miami*, five episodes, |

	don't even like it, fell asleep, the dreams again, woke up –
Holly	I had a dream too, the same thing . . . Monsters, an explosion. It's the weather. Apparently it happens in February? Because people are stuck inside, in their jobs doing the same kind of things with the same kind of problems, so we all have similar dreams.
Mark	It's June.

He drinks his coffee.

You getting up then Mowgli? Work to do. You mind fifties?

How's the course going?

She shrugs as he puts some money down and goes out.

Hope it's worth it.

Five

Dennis, **Ruby** and **Sarah** *are having breakfast.*

Sarah	Ruby tell your father what you're doing at school.
Ruby	Dinosaurs.
Dennis	Dinosaurs? That's great. I love dinosaurs.
Ruby	Yeah.
Dennis	Like *The Flintstones*!
Ruby	I beg your pardon?
Dennis	You know. Fred Flintstone, Barney Rubble. We used to watch it munchkin, you remember?

Ruby	It's not like *The Flintstones* at all. The fossil record shows that humans and dinosaurs never existed at the same time.

Sarah *drops her knife on her plate.*

Dennis	Well sure honey but it's a cartoon.
Ruby	I know.
Dennis	These Flintstones, they go to the movies, they have cars powered with their feet, I don't think the fossil record has much to say about that either.
Ruby	Yeah.
Dennis	But it's okay, because it's a story. It's not real.
Ruby	Then it's not like what I studied at school, is it?
Dennis	Well.
Ruby	What I studied at school is fact.
Sarah	You see what I mean?
Dennis	Honey –
Sarah	She's like this with me all the time.
Ruby	Like what?

Dennis *finishes his breakfast. Puts his napkin down on the table.*

Dennis	Have you read books?
Ruby	I'm always reading books.
Dennis	I mean fiction.
Ruby	Yeah.
Dennis	What?
Ruby	. . .

Dennis	What about . . . Harry Potter! Have you read that?
Ruby	Yes.
Dennis	Did you like it?
Ruby	No.
Dennis	Why?
Ruby	It was stupid.
Dennis	Well that's the idea. It's like using your imagination. It's not real. That's the point.
Ruby	I know what fiction is. I don't mean imaginary I mean it's stupid. It's not intelligent. It's for children.
Dennis	Well sure but your mother and me –
Ruby	Really stupid children who only understand short words like 'cat' and 'apple' and 'house'
Dennis	Your mother and me, we like it – the story's interesting. It takes us out of the real world and shows us something else, something more that makes the real world better. Maybe you should give it another go? It's fun.
Ruby	Dad? Have you seen what's going on? A man kills seventy people with a gun, hundreds of protestors executed by the Syrian government, thousands of children starving in the Horn of Africa. There's evil Dad. There's so much evil in the world. I don't have time for fun.

Six

The park. Green open space. People milling about. It's a weekday,
so not that busy.

Zia *is with* **Fiona**.

Zia	What about Friday?
Fiona	I'm sorry?
Zia	We could go out on Friday? There's this new film, it's a documentary about the larger asteroids. Some of them are bigger than the planets and they reckon that –
Fiona	Listen –
Zia	– instead of manned missions to Mars next, we might go to one of them, some of them might have ice, water, maybe life, what do you think? I know it sounds geeky but it's good and we can get popcorn.
Fiona	It's not working.
Zia	Pepsi.
Fiona	I don't want to see you again.
Zia	Shit load of nachos. What?
Fiona	Zia. We don't get on.
Zia	Yeah we do.
Fiona	No.
Zia	I do.
Fiona	Exactly.
Zia	Oh.

Beat.

Fiona	I want to call it a day.

Zia	Why?
Fiona	Zia –
Zia	Cos you can't just say that say it's not working and leave it like that you can't – okay give me one proper reason yeah?
Fiona	The shouting. In your sleep. It wakes me up.
Zia	Oh. Right. The shouting.
Fiona	Yeah.
Zia	Yeah. Well.

Fiona *turns to leave –*

Zia	Wait! Please. Wait a –

John *arrives, places the bucket on the ground and stands on it.*

John	Okay okay okay.

Zia *turns, at first irritated, then starts to listen.*

John	I know this is weird and you're having a good time but I've had a thought about a battery hen.

Fiona *leaves*

John	Okay. So this hen has lived in this box her whole life. She's never seen anything else. She just sits there and the food arrives and the eggs get taken away. Now of course her brain is much smaller than ours but I'd like to imagine she has some thoughts on her situation.
	What would she think about the world?
	She hears noises, so she thinks there are others outside. On the evidence she's got, she'd probably assume these are other

chickens. She's unlikely to work out that her keepers are people – she'd have no concept of us, the world, the ground, the sun or the moon. Limited by what she could sense, and what her brain could deduce, she would get it all very, very wrong.

Alice *crosses the park, watches for a moment, and leaves.*

John   My thought was that, like that hen, we go around thinking eventually we'll work everything out – but limited by what we can sense and what we can deduce, surely it's possible there are things that leave no evidence and no trace? That we have no concept of.

So when people say they are sure that there can't be a God, even when they say that's its unlikely, they're like a battery hen denying the existence of the moon. They can't know. None of us can, for sure. What was there before the universe? What happens when we die?

Rob *hears this . . .*

Liam *crosses the park, stops to listen to* **John**.

John   It's all open.

Same time tomorrow.

A slightly embarrassed silence. **Liam** *walks off.* **John** *gets down off the bucket and picks it up.* **Rob** *approaches him, nervous – distracted.* **Holly** *hangs around.*

Rob   Hi. Are you – from a group – an organisation?

John   No. Just me.

Rob	I'm . . . going away – we're all heading off and . . .
	Have you got a book?
John	No.
Rob	A leaflet?
John	I'm here tomorrow.
Rob	I'm going away.
Holly	I'll film it.
Rob	What?
Holly	I'll film it tomorrow, put it online, then you can watch it, yeah?
Rob	Oh. Right. Thanks.
Holly	What's your name?
John	John.
Holly	John in the park. That's what I'll call it.
Rob	Right. Thanks.

He goes.

Holly	I'm Holly by the way.
John	Good to meet you.

*They shake hands and she goes, leaving **Zia**.*

Zia	Have you heard about the graph?
John	What?
Zia	There's this graph and if you plot scientific progress against time you see it's an exponential curve. The rate of progress doubles every ten years and if you plot this curve it gets to a point where it's a straight line, which would

technically mean infinite progress in a single moment. According to the graph it is going to happen in ten years. This moment. The singularity.

Thought it was interesting. Sorry, I'm a bit – my girlfriend just left me.

Apparently I'm shouting, at night and . . . It puts them off.

Tomorrow yeah?

John   Yeah.

Seven

A large table, around which are gathered, for a briefing – **Sir Christopher** (*Head of the Armed Forces*), **Dennis** *and* **Ruth**, *who's with* **Carol**, **Martin** *and* **Liam**.

Carol	The Head of the Armed Forces Prime Minister –
Ruth	Sir Christopher thank you for coming. Always nice to have a uniform in the building, engenders some much-needed formality in the ranks don't you think Carol?
Sir Christopher	Glad to be of service.
Ruth	This is Dennis Harrison.
Dennis	Sir Christopher, good to meet you.
Sir Christopher	You're from the embassy.
Ruth	Dennis is working with us on this. He's close to the president. Shall we make a start?

Martin	Everyone's been given the background to look over –
Sir Christopher	Good because in the past political advisors have been strangely uninformed –
Ruth	Liam, are you strangely uninformed about Iran?
Liam	I worked in Arab countries for five years?
Sir Christopher	Iran isn't an Arab country.
Liam	Well . . .
Sir Christopher	This is what I mean.
Ruth	Very good. Liam, read the file. Sir Christopher?
Sir Christopher	Three months ago, Iran pulled out of the Nuclear Non-proliferation Treaty. The withdrawal is a clear sign the regime has the intention and potentially the technology to develop a nuclear weapon – which of course, would change everything – the ability of the regime to act against it's own people with impunity, the balance of power with Israel. It would also allow the fundamentalist religious faction in Iran to propagate their anti-Semitic and anti-western agenda with even more vigour. But our biggest concern is terrorism. If nuclear material and technology fell into the hands of a terrorist group, it would destabilise the entire civilised world.
Dennis	What terrorist group?
Sir Christopher	I beg your pardon?
Dennis	Can we be specific?

Sir Christopher	Iran funds and supports enemy factions in Iraq and Afghanistan. Their money kills our soldiers.
Dennis	But no links with Al-Qaeda.
Sir Christopher	No.
Dennis	I'm just clarifying because when you say terrorism –
Sir Christopher	I'm sure the Prime Minister understands the difference – Prime Minister, perhaps we should have this meeting on our own –
Dennis	The prime minister likes perspective.
Sir Christopher	Yes. That's what I provide.
Dennis	You have an opinion.
Sir Christopher	And you don't?
Ruth	Of course he does. That's what I want. Opinions. Both of you.
Sir Christopher	Alright – the U.S military is looking at an initial campaign potentially beginning in approximately four weeks time. We concur with the Americans that anything less than a full-scale occupation would have little effect to the nuclear programme, in fact it may simply encourage them to speed it up.
Ruth	There's not a way of standing back? Providing military support for some kind of . . . homegrown / revolution?
Sir Christopher	Much too slow and unreliable I'm afraid. No, the only way to do it is to get in the country quickly and physically dismantle every last piece.

Ruth   All or nothing.

Sir Christopher That's correct.

Fractional beat.

Liam   Can I . . . ?

Ruth   Liam?

Liam   The British people will ask why we're
                    spending millions on a war a long way
                    away when their hospital's in crisis, the
                    library is closed and their son can't go
                    to university. They will protest in their
                    thousands. I don't know if you could
                    survive it.

Sir Christopher The public don't have the long view,
                    Prime Minister, that's why they elected
                    you. If we get this wrong, there will be
                    serious consequences for decades to
                    come. We've tried everything else but the
                    Iranian intentions are clear. They want
                    the bomb.

Dennis   They want respect. It's not so long ago
                    Britain and America were funding a war
                    against them. So we're trying to build up
                    trust.

Sir Christopher Your talks. How are they going?

Dennis   They're going well.

Sir Christopher My counterparts at the Pentagon don't
                    have much hope. A waste of time. That's
                    what they said.

Dennis   That remains to be seen.

Beat

Ruth   If we did it. Casualties?

Sir Christopher	Minimum.
Ruth	Not just our troops. I mean in total, the invasion, the aftermath, Iranian, American, British, if we proceed, how many people would die?
Sir Christopher	Prime Minister I'm reluctant to confidently predict –
Ruth	Sir Christopher, in the end I may well have to pick up that phone and condemn a large number of people to death, so is it not reasonable to ask if you know roughly what that number will be?
Sir Christopher	Of course, but –
Ruth	A hundred? Five hundred? Five thousand?
Sir Christopher	We'd hope that the Iranians themselves would welcome action like this and -
Dennis	A hundred thousand. That's what they're telling me. On previous experience, assuming this will take years to achieve, over a hundred thousand dead.

Beat.

Prime Minister, the talks are progressing. We sincerely hope this will all be academic.

Beat.

Ruth	Keep me updated. Thank you everyone. Carol – give me the room for a minute, yes?

*They go, leaving **Ruth** on her own.*

*We hear the sound of a hoover . . . **Shannon** enters.*

Shannon	Oh hello!
Ruth	No.
	No!
	Not. Now. Go.
	Go away.

Shannon *looks at her, leaves the hoover running, a strange moment.*

Then she takes off her apron, throws it on the ground, and leaves.

Ruth *goes across, slowly, and switches the hoover off.*

Eight

Amir *is watching a video of* **John** *on a laptop.*

John	We've given up and now we wave it all through – class, inequality, unkindness, we glamorise violence, lust after infinite riches, and we all feel it but the question is why?

Rachel *comes in.* **Amir** *stays watching the video.* **Rachel** *goes to switch on the lamp.*

Amir	Alright?

The lamp doesn't work. **Amir** *doesn't see.*

	Good day?

He keeps watching the video.

Rachel	I really don't want to be the boring one?
Amir	What?
Rachel	Pause it.
Amir	What? Oh –

He stops the video.

Rachel	Thank you I really don't want to be the boring one and I know we're in very different places at the moment in our lives – you've been on the internet all day reading the *Guardian* website, watching your videos – how's John getting on?
Amir	Good – people are starting to write about what he's doing –
Rachel	Yeah and you've been posting and tweeting and all of that and you've had a nice day which is good but I've got work, and this is the bit where I really don't want to be the boring one in this relationship but did you call about the washing machine?
Amir	Okay –
Rachel	Did you pick up the shopping?
Amir	. . .
Rachel	Do the light bulbs? Well no we can see the answer to that.
Amir	I just got . . . I've got into this. Have you watched him? Have you actually sat down and heard what he's got to say?
Rachel	When would I have time to do that?

Beat.

Amir	Rach, we've always talked – look I know this sounds a bit mad – but we've talked ever since university about the moment when something changes, and John's saying these things, and . . . you know . . . he's open, he's passionate and he means it. And it's only just started, but people are listening because he's taking everyone out

of all of this – exactly what you're talking about our little houses and things we buy and washing machines and light bulbs and he's making them feel like there could be something more.

Rachel   Have you left the sofa today?

Amir   . . .

Rachel   What?

Beat.

Rachel   Anyway. I *like* our house. What's wrong with our house?

Amir *looks at her, a bit crushed.* **John** *enters.*

Rachel   John, we were just talking about you. Had a good day? Amir's saying you're becoming famous.

John   You've been working hard.

Rachel   Yeah I have.

John   That's good.

    But I think you should stop now.

Rachel   What?

John   For the evening. Stop.

Rachel   Stop what – what are you talking about, weird abstract instructions. What, is my energy a bit high at the moment, you're going to sort out my *chakra*. Okay. I'll stop. What? What now?

Beat.

    Shall we do a *trust exercise*?

John   You find it difficult, don't you?

Rachel	I . . . No.

Beat.

	What?
John	See?
Rachel	Oh fuck off John.

John *smiles – he knows her.*

John	I've done the shopping. Got everything we need.
	I'll cook tonight. You put your feet up.
Amir	I was going to get it.
John	No. It's fine. You two stay there. My turn.

He goes.

Amir *and* **Rachel** *sit for a moment.*

Then as **Edith** *starts playing,* **Rachel** *pulls the laptop over and starts to watch the video.*

Nine

Edith *goes to the piano. There's a cross on the top.*

She begins to play a tune. 'The Only Girl in the World' by Rihanna

As she does, **Sarah** *appears outside her house, smoking.*

Scene Ten

Morning. **Sarah** *is smoking outside her house. She sees* **John** *walking past.*

Sarah	Hey!

John *looks up and walks over.*

John	Hello

Sarah	It's you. Isn't it? From the airport.
John	Yes. I'm sorry. I was a mess then, wasn't I? I think I scared your daughter.
Sarah	No. She should be apologising. Everything scares her.
John	She's a little girl.
Sarah	Even smoking. That's why I have to stand out here.
	I'm Sarah.
John	John.
Sarah	Hi John.
Beat.	
John	Is this your house?
Sarah	It's the property of the US government. My husband. I think it's a prison. What are you up to?
John	I'm going to the park. Every day I go, I speak for a while, then we sit and talk about things.
Sarah	Who's we?
John	Anyone who's around.
Sarah	That sounds nice.
John	You should come. We start at one o'clock.
Sarah	I'm not supposed to leave the house on my own. We're high security. If I want to go shopping I make a phone call and they send these men round. All dressed in black. They look after us.
John	Maybe you could sneak away? Come with me.

Sarah	Maybe.

Beat.

John	Last time, you weren't sleeping.
Sarah	The dreams.
John	How are they now?

She looks at him.

Sarah	Do you believe in God John?
John	I believe there's something, yes.
Sarah	Do you think sometimes, you have to go with your instinct, sometimes if you know something is right, you have to do it, even if everyone around you thinks you're mad?
John	Sometimes you have to do what you believe to be right.
Sarah	Yes.
John	If it's important.

She looks at him for a second. Offers him a cigarette.

Sarah	Do you want one of these?
John	No thank you. I should go.
Sarah	You know it wasn't the smell that she had a problem with.
	I think she could tell you were good.
	A good man. And she didn't like it.
John	Bye Sarah.
Sarah	Bye.

Eleven

The park. Light, green grass, blue sky. A slightly bigger crowd, sat and stood around the bucket. **Zia**, **Shannon** *and* **Holly** *are there. Also in the crowd is* **Martin**, *on his lunchbreak. Half-way through the speech,* **Mark** *turns up to watch.*

John	There are things we want. We want the very best healthcare and education, free at the point of use, for all. We want to narrow the gap between rich and poor, both here, and across the world. But with these things we are told – this is just not how the world works anymore. You are naive if you think any of it is possible.
	So we shrug and walk away, and learn instead the comfort of the downbeat, the safety of irony and pessimism. We sleepwalk from weekend to weekend, looking forward to the simple comforts. We earn we buy, we live we die, we earn we buy, this, we are told, is enough – central heating, delivery shopping, bread and circuses, wine and HBO.

Stephen *walks by, notices what's going on, and stops to watch.*

John	Well I want you to remove the barriers and believe that these may be the facts on the ground but the ground can be changed – to work out what you want and go for it with all your conviction and don't care if you seem outrageous or stupid. Believe in God, believe in each other, in progress or science or whatever you want but through believing in the impossible you might just make it happen. All that's needed, in the end, is belief.

John *steps off the bucket.* **Stephen** *approaches* **John**.

Stephen	So.
John	Stephen.
Stephen	I live in Notting Hill, I walk into town, I attend my meeting, then on ambling back I see this group of people gathered together, reminding me of the political rallies of my youth, I go to investigate and . . . oh look!
	A resurrection.
	Of sorts.
	Where have you been John?
	It did you no good. Disappearing like that. Made you look guilty. And your friends . . . well.
John	Do you think it's going to rain?
Stephen	It was a selfish thing to do. Don't you think? I mean I personally, I would call it a number of things far worse than that, but at the very least it was selfish, to abandon everyone. Don't you agree?

*As **Stephen** carries on, **John** puts his hand out – no rain . . .*

Stephen	Is this what you're up to? Since you've come back. Preaching.
John	Your eyes are red.
Stephen	It happens at my age. What are you here to talk about? God?
John	
Stephen	Does Ruth know? That you're back. Have you told her?
	No. Of course you haven't.

Holly *comes over with a clipboard.*

Holly	Hello.
John	Holly, this is Stephen Crossley he used to be my lecturer at university, taught me a lot. Stephen famously doesn't believe in God, in fact he thinks belief is dangerous, not just organised religion but *belief itself.* He goes around claiming that there 'probably isn't a God' which considering almost any definition of a divine being is a weirdly unintellectual and totally unprovable statement to make, and if there's one thing Stephen objects to it's things you can't prove. But he's a good man. And he can drink a lot. Holly's collecting email addresses, she's started a website, and she has sex for money.
Holly	What? Shut up.
John	You said you're fine with it.
Holly	Yeah I am.
John	Well then.

John *puts his hand out. Still no rain.* **Zia**'s *in the background.*

Stephen	John, let me give you her number.

Shannon *interrupts as* **Stephen** *writes on a piece of paper.*

Shannon	Hi.
Stephen	Let me give you her number.
Shannon	Sorry, to interrupt – oops – I'm Shannon, I've been watching the other speeches – thought I'd come down and see for myself.
John	Hi

Shannon	I just wanted to say . . . they're really . . . I've quit my job! I think you're right. We have to do something important.
Stephen	You've quit your job?
Shannon	I hated my boss.
Stephen	How do you do it John?
Shannon	I beg your pardon?
Stephen	These people – she quit her job? The way things are at the moment – who does that?
Shannon	I am here.
Stephen	What is all this? The park. The speeches. Your little friends. What are you up to?
John	Have you had bad dreams?
Stephen	. . .

John *looks at him.*

John	Oh.
	Hang on . . .

Thunder and it starts to rain. Everyone gets umbrellas and coats out.

Stephen, *unimpressed, writes a number down.*

Stephen	This is her personal number – you'll get straight through.
	Call her.

He walks away. **John** *leaves with* **Zia** *and* **Shannon**, *as* **Holly** *puts her hood up and tries to sort out her phone.*

Mark *is there.*

Mark	You haven't answered my calls. You're here every day. I see you on my

	lunchbreak. Going round with your . . . clipboard.
	Why didn't you get back to me?
Holly	I don't . . .
Mark	You don't . . . what?
Holly	What we do. I don't like it.
Mark	What? – You don't like it – Then why didn't you say?
Holly	I was scared.
Mark	Of what?
Holly	Of you.
Mark	. . .

John *comes over with an umbrella.*

Mark	Oh. Hello. Good. Saw your speech.
Holly	Mark –
Mark	Saw the website too. Funny. It is supposed to be funny right?
Holly	Just fuck off yeah this isn't anything to do with you.
John	It's okay.
Mark	What?
John	Really. Mark. It's okay.
Mark	Right. I need to get back to the office. You know. Job. Money.
	Holly. Call me yeah?

He looks at **John**. *Something unnerving, which he ignores.*

He goes off, into the rain. **Holly** *turns to* **John**, *on the point of tears, in the rain. Just the two of them.*

13

A pause.

John   Are you alright?

She isn't. **John** *opens the umbrella and she hugs him underneath, and cries.*

Twelve

In **Ruth**'s *Number 10 flat.* **Stephen** *enters.* **Ruth** *is getting ready.*

Ruth   This better be important. I'm late and
                     then there's a call saying that the famous
                     atheist Stephen Crossley has just turned up
                     at Number 10. The press all saw you walk
                     in. What's going on?

Stephen   I thought you'd want to know.

Ruth   What?

Stephen   John's come back. I saw him.

Beat.

                     I gave him your number. Said he should
                     call you.

Ruth   What number?

Stephen   Your number, your personal number.

Ruth *looks at a phone on the side.*

Ruth   I'm . . . I'm late.

                     I'm really . . .

                     I have to go . . .

She slams the side of her dressing table, hard. Angry.

She looks out the window. The rain pours down hard.

                     Is it me, or is getting darker?

Thirteen

Sarah *is chopping vegetables in the kitchen. Tense. The rain outside.* **Ruby** *enters reading her Kindle.*

Sarah	It's bedtime.
Ruby	I'm reading.
Sarah	You've read enough.
Ruby	I'm nearly at the end.
Sarah	You can finish it in bed.
Ruby	I don't want to finish it in bed, once you get to bed you start to fall asleep, I want to think about this.
Sarah	. . . .
Ruby	Mom, do you read books?
Sarah	Of course.
Ruby	I never see you. What was the last book you read?

Sarah *chops.*

Ruby	What do you do?
Sarah	I'm your mommy.
Ruby	But what do you do for a living?
Sarah	I run a charity.
Ruby	On Thursdays.
Sarah	Yes.
Ruby	In the afternoons on Thursdays.
Sarah	. . .
Ruby	Between two and four-thirty.
Sarah	. . .

| **Ruby** | I'm reading a book about emancipation and it seems to me that it's okay for women to go out in the world and make something of themselves, in fact it seems to me that that's a good thing and it's been fought for by generations of women in the past, but you don't do that, you stay in most of the time with me, and even when I'm at school you're still here. |

Sarah *chops*.

Ruby	Maybe if you read books it would take you out of yourself. You know what E.M. Forster says in *A Room with a View*?
Sarah	Ruby . . .
Ruby	We read to know we're not alone.
Sarah	It's your bedtime.
Ruby	No.
Sarah	I've had enough.
Ruby	You should read.
Sarah	I'm not alone.
Ruby	You don't like me asking questions.
Sarah	It's time to listen to your mommy.
Ruby	I think questioning makes us who we are.
Sarah	You're not a good child, are you?
Ruby	Why don't you like me asking questions Mom?
Sarah	You're not *good*
Ruby	You always get angry when I ask questions.

Sarah *chops. Chops.*

Ruby   Is it possible for a daughter to be cleverer
                      than her mother?

Sarah *stops chopping and looks at* **Ruby**.

The neon light above flickers. Strobes.

                      Mom?

*The cupboard door opens in the kitchen and an emaciated figure all
in black slowly emerges.*

                      Mom!

Ruby *starts screaming as the figure grabs her. She kicks and
screams as he drags her into the cupboard. The moment the door
is shut again, the kitchen returns to normal.* **Sarah** *carries on
chopping.*

Slow fade to black.

Act Three

One

We again hear Laurie Anderson – 'Someone Else's Dream'.

This time it's cut even shorter.

The twelve wake up again, as before, terrified and breathing.

Two

Music plays. **Edith** *stares straight forward – terrified, in a trance – we're not sure . . .*

Mark *and* **Alice** *enter.*

Mark	Edith the door was open.

He sees her.

	Edith?
Edith	Oh. Mark. Didn't hear you. Going a bit deaf.
Mark	They're going to drop the case.
Edith	What?
Mark	They're going to drop the case.
Edith	I'm a bit deaf . . .
Mark	They're going to drop the case!
Edith	Is this your girlfriend?
Mark	Oh for Christ's –
Alice	I'm Alice. Mark's assistant. We spoke on the phone.
Edith	Do you have a girlfriend?
Mark	Look we're in a bit of a hurry.

Edith	My granddaughter Holly, she's your age.
Mark	I know, she's the one who –
Edith	But she's black. You might have a problem with that.
Mark	No.
Edith	Some white guys get scared by black girls that's what she told me.
Mark	The bank have been persuaded to stop.
Edith	What did you tell them?
Mark	They thought this was your house.
Edith	I rent it.
Mark	I know but they thought it was yours. When I proved to them that wasn't the case, they said they'd let it go, on one condition.
Edith	Maybe you should go out with Alice. She seems like a nice girl.
Alice	He's not my type.
Mark	Can we concentrate?
Edith	You know Mark, there was a time when the high street bank wouldn't sue an old woman for all she was worth.
Mark	You threw a shopping trolley through their window.
Edith	They did far worse to me.
Mark	Yes, look –
Edith (*to* **Alice**)	I was stood in that queue for half an hour and my legs were hurting and there were no chairs and no one was helping, and I

asked for help but no one did anything,
they just thought I was mad, so I left, and
I was going to change to another bank
but then I realised I couldn't because
I've got a terrible credit rating because
of the overdraft charges they made and I
was walking down that road and all these
young people were out protesting and
rioting and I thought good for them – I
thought, I've had enough so there was a
trolley yes and I picked it up and put it
through their window, the money they've
taken off me more than makes up for it, I
hate that bank. It's shit. It's a shit bank.

NatWest. It was NatWest if you want to
know.

She goes to her computer.

Mark	Edith you're not allowed in any branch from now on.
Edith	Suits me. Do you wear those shoes to work?
Alice	Yes I do.
Edith	Shoes say a lot about a person dear.
Alice	Really?
Edith	And your shoes say I'm a fucking idiot don't take me seriously whatever you do. How much are you charging me then?
Mark	We'll send you an invoice.
Edith	I found a plate I can put on eBay, that's a start . . .
Alice	Mark . . .
Mark	Alright, call it a favour . . .

Edith	What?
Mark	Don't worry about the money.
Edith	If only. Here we are!
	Money yes, none of that, I thought the world was going to hell in a handcart, another Thatcher making everything worse and worse but then my granddaughter showed me this. She's been making these videos.
Mark	Oh don't tell me –
Edith	It's this man. He goes into the park and he stands there and speaks and look.
	Look how many people have been watching. Thousands. That's where she is now.
	I like him.
	His names' John.

Three

Dennis *arrives back at the house. He has a suitcase.* **Sarah** *is in her dressing gown, watching something on a laptop.*

Dennis	Hey!
Sarah	Hey.

She closes the laptop down.

Sarah	How was the flight?
Dennis	Aargh. Red eye.
Sarah	Toast?
Dennis	Toast! Good.

Sarah *starts slicing bread with a knife and puts the bread into a toaster.*

Dennis	Missed you. How's Munchkin? Where is she?
Sarah	In bed. Reading. She's never off that thing you gave her.
Dennis	She's a good kid.
Sarah	Here.
Dennis	What?
Sarah	Coffee?
Dennis	Oh. Thanks. Still in bed?
	Doesn't she have . . . what is it? *Ballet* this morning?
Sarah	She didn't want to go.
Dennis	Really?
Sarah	Last night she said don't get me up I want to stay in bed in the morning and read.
Dennis	She likes ballet.
Sarah	Well then you have a conversation with her Dennis, if you don't trust me, that I've done my best, why don't you go in there and ask her?

The toast pops. **Sarah** *butters it.*

Dennis	Hey.
Sarah	What?
Dennis	. . . .
Sarah	There.

She gives him the toast. He takes a bite.

Dennis	Thanks.
	Still the dreams?

Sarah	. . .
Dennis	You should take those pills.
Sarah	They don't help.

Pause. **Dennis** *eats another slice of toast. Looks at his watch.*

Dennis	Hell. I have to go.
Sarah	How are things at work? Is everything . . . OK?
Dennis	. . .
Sarah	. . .
Dennis	I love you. We'll all catch up tonight.

He kisses her and goes with his toast. **Sarah** *stares for a moment. Then goes, opens the computer, and presses play on what she was watching.*

Four

The park. **Zia** *and* **Shannon***, and others, wait for* **John***.*

They coyly watch each other, eventually striking up a conversation –

Zia	Thirteen.
Shannon	What?
Zia	If you go through his speeches and you count the letters in the right way you get the number thirteen, again and again.
Shannon	You've tried it?
Zia	People have yeah, cos thirteen's unlucky in almost every culture. Apparently there's these insects and they live underground and only come out every thirteen years, cos thirteen's the least likely mathematically to coincide with other insects' breeding patterns.

Shannon	This on the internet?
Zia	Yeah.
Shannon	Thought so.

John *enters with his bucket. A* **Heckler** *is nearby and enthusiastic.*
As **John**'s *about to speak –*

Heckler	Talk about Iran!
John	I . . . what?
Heckler	Well they're saying it's all going to kick off soon, so what do you think about that then?
Holly	No . . . he – let him talk –
Heckler	Come on!
	What do you think?

John *looks at the* **Heckler**. *Then steps off the bucket and goes.*

| **Heckler** | What? |
| | Where's he going? |

Holly *goes after him.*

Shannon	See ya then.
Zia	Right.
	Do you want to . . . come round mine. Tonight. I've got a telescope.
Shannon	I beg your pardon?
Zia	It's new. I saved up. To look at the – you know – stars. So. We could.
Shannon	Yeah.
Zia	Do that.
Shannon	Okay.

Zia	If you want?
Shannon	Yeah.
Zia	What?
Shannon	Yeah.
Zia	You will?
Shannon	Yeah.
Zia	Shit.
	Good.

Beat.

Zia	Do you know anything about it?
Shannon	What?
Zia	Iran.
Shannon	Not really.

Five

Stephen *is making a speech at the Oxford Union.*

Stephen   Ladies and Gentlemen, the Iranian regime is, simply put, brutal. They have clung onto power, rigged elections, kidnapped, tortured, repressed, and murdered their own people in their thousands, and have been shown to actively support terrorist organisations.

As you may imagine, the regime is deeply unpopular with the majority of Iranians, who are, by and large, young, educated and desperate to choose their own future. These young people know what they are missing, how their freedoms are curtailed. They are desperate to put an end to this

13

oppression but their voices are silenced
and their numbers reduced through
imprisonment, torture and death. And
let us not forget, as the mullahs have, to
consider the women. The women here
tonight, if you were Iranian, would be
possessions. If, as a woman, you cheated
on your husband, you would be stoned to
death. If you are interested and want to
see a woman being stoned to death then
I direct you to the internet where ladies
and gentlemen, you will find a number
of videos – but I give you a warning – it is
utterly horrific and it takes her a very long
time to die.

Six

A split scene – **Ruth** *and* **Dennis** *in her office.* **Amir** *and* **Rachel**
at home.

Ruth	How was the trip?
Dennis	Good.
Ruth	You spoke to the President?
Dennis	Yes.
Amir	Yeah.
Ruth	What did he say?
Rachel	Just take a minute, take a minute to breath, cos I can't believe –
Dennis	You've read the transcripts, I'm sure your people have spoken to you.
Amir	I don't need a minute.
Dennis	The feeling in Washington is that these talks were always just stalling for time.

Amir	I know what I think.
Dennis	The President's had enough.
Amir	It's like everything John's been saying.
Rachel	John? No. John's not here, let's stay on you.
Dennis	He feels this is the moment.
Amir	We should do it.
Rachel	War?
Ruth	I see.
Amir	Yes.
Dennis	Yes.

Beat.

Amir	This is an opportunity. You haven't been there. You're not allowed to speak your mind, the punishments the regime hands out are medieval –
Rachel	Well if that's the criteria / there's a long list of other countries.
Dennis	You'll talk to him yourself but the President asked me to come and speak to you tonight. To test the water.
Amir	Government sanctioned gangs pulling people out of cars for not dressing correctly, doctors, academics arrested for speaking out
Dennis	He wonders how you're feeling.
Ruth	How I'm feeling?
Dennis	That's right.

Amir	– and there are young people like us sat in rooms like this watching TV and they'll be praying we go in and help them.
Rachel	You've got family out there – you want them bombed?
Ruth	How I'm *feeling*?
Rachel	You want to throw the country into civil war?
Amir	It's exactly what John says about purpose. I've had enough of sitting back and letting them –
Rachel	Well you would know about sitting back.
Ruth	I give an order, and then within hours, people are dead.
Amir	I thought you believed in the rights of women.
Rachel	Of course –
Amir	But only in this country –
Rachel	I'm not sure a genocidal war will benefit women in any country particularly, but seeing as you know so much about women and their rights –
Ruth	I don't want to go to war, Dennis, but if it's necessary –
Amir	When did you start talking to me like this?
Ruth	I absolutely will.
Amir	When did you entirely lose respect?
Ruth	So how am I *feeling*?
Rachel	I don't know.

Ruth	Ambivalent.
Dennis	Right.
Amir	Right.
Rachel	But . . . since you ask, it's probably to do with what you're advocating, John wouldn't want this, no one we know would want this – massive invasion and occupation of a country that hasn't attacked us, hundreds of thousands dead,
Amir	The people I know over there are ready for sacrifice –
Rachel	But this isn't them fighting this is us, with troops and planes that flatten blocks and villages – Amir I don't even know where / to start if you're stupid or naïve or right-wing, we went on the *anti-war march* remember you shouting all the way –
Amir	No, no, you can't shut up you're talking and being clever and sneering all the fucking time but you never think really *think* about anything – you wonder why I wake up in the night screaming it's nothing to do with what's going on there, it's probably being next to you all night, this stuff in your head, all your *problems*.
Dennis	Ruth.
Ruth	I'm sorry?
Dennis	Can I call you Ruth?
Amir	John was right.
Rachel	What?
Dennis	May I speak freely?

Amir	You talk and shout and tell people what to do but you never listen really, you never – just – stop.
Rachel	I . . .
Ruth	Yes?
Dennis	Do you have anyone?
Ruth	What?
Dennis	Anyone you can talk to, about how you feel, because from what I see . . . can I say this? From what I see, you're on your own, and under a lot of pressure.
	Everyone knows you've been through a lot. And these people you're surrounded by, your advisors, I don't know how much they understand . . . If you needed someone to . . . To talk to . . .
Rachel	Alright then.
Amir	What?
Dennis	I think we get on.

Ruth *stares at him.*

Amir	What?

Martin *enters.*

Martin	Mr Harrison. There's a call for you.
	Your wife.
	Apparently it's urgent.
Dennis	I'm sorry. Prime Minister, we could talk about the options.
Rachel	Yes. Let's stop. You and me. Tonight.

Ruth	Dennis. Thank you for the offer and you're right, I'm under a lot of pressure, but I think I'm coping with it all quite well considering my emotional state and the fact I'm a woman and everything.
Amir	That's not what I . . .
Dennis	That's not what I meant.
Ruth	When the time comes, I'll make my decision.
	I know what you meant.
	Talk to your wife.

Dennis *turns and enters the kitchen where* **Sarah** *is sat, smoking.*

Ruth *stays for a while, then leaves.*

Amir	Rachel –
Rachel	Yes.
	Yes.
	Let's put an end to it.

Seven

Dennis*'s house.* **Sarah** *is sat smoking at the kitchen table.* **Dennis** *enters. Slowly. Devastated.*

Dennis	They say there's been no forced entry to the house.
Sarah	So where's she gone? Why would she do this to us? We look after her. I'm frightened –
Dennis	If she had any sense of anything it was responsibility, she understood that what

	we do affects other people. She wouldn't run away.
Sarah	We should call her friends.
Dennis	They don't know anything.
Sarah	Oh God oh God. Shouldn't you be at work?
Dennis	Honey, our daughter –
Sarah	But it's important.
Dennis	Our daughter has gone. I'm not doing anything else until we find her.
Sarah	Why?
Dennis	What?
Sarah	Why has this happened? To us. Didn't I treat her right?

Dennis *looks at* **Sarah***, without an answer.*

Sarah	Pray.
Dennis	She'll be okay.
Sarah	Pray with me.

Sarah *puts her cigarette out and shuts her eyes.* **Dennis** *looks at her then does the same.*

Sarah	Please . . . God.

Eight

It's getting later now. Night. Stars.

A choral singer starts. Baroque.

As **Sarah** *prays we see* **Mark** *coming back to his flat with some booze and cigarettes, and* **Alice***, who's a bit drunk. He lights cigarettes, pours drink, ignores* **Alice***.*

Sarah	God, save us, save us from darkness, save us from damnation.

Edith *puts on her iPod and goes out running.*

Sarah	Save us from evil, from the end, from death and pain . . .

Zia *and* **Shannon** *are out with a telescope looking at the stars.* **Shannon** *smokes.* **Holly***, with an iPod, calls* **Edith***.*

John *appears, walking through all of them.*

Shannon	That one . . .
Sarah	From the end.
Shannon	It looks like a hand, reaching out.
Sarah	Save us from what we fear, guide us to salvation,
Zia	You ever wonder what's at the edge?
Sarah	. . . show us how to live.
Shannon	The edge of what?
Sarah	. . . show us the light.
Zia	The universe.
Edith	Hello?
Holly	Gran? He's gone.
Edith	Who? Who's gone?
Zia	You know it's actually quite likely that there are an infinite number of parallel universes where each possibility that could ever happen is played out. Every possibility.
Shannon	You say this stuff to all the girls?
Zia	Er . . . yeah. I do actually.

| **Mark** | Come on then. |

| **Shannon** | I think that's where you go wrong. |

The phone is ringing. **Ruth** *looks at it. Then answers it.*

Ruth	Hello?
	Yes.
	I . . .

John *enters.*

| **Ruth** | I can't – |

She hangs up, then unplugs the phone from the socket. Over the next page, she walks to the centre of the stage and closes her eyes. **Alice** *and* **Mark** *start to kiss.* **Martin** *arrives with a pile of papers to sort through.*

Rob *packs his kit bag.* **Stephen** *continues his speech from earlier* . . .

| **John** | Today I've read papers, watched the television. |

| **Stephen** | You may think I'm alarmist, that I'm exaggerating. |

| **John** | I've seen the pictures we all have. Heard what's being said – |

| **Shannon** | They all think I'm stupid. |

| **Zia** | I don't. |

| **John** | They tell us, if we do nothing, it's a risk. |

| **Stephen** | When I imagine what might happen in the years to come, what terrifies me the most? |

| **Mark** | Stop. |

| **Stephen** | A thermo-nuclear theocracy. |

Stephen *coughs.* **Mark** *has pushed* **Alice** *off.*

John	So instead, they say, we have to go in, and stop them.
Alice	What's the problem?
Holly	Gran?
Mark	Go. Get out. Get out!
John	The army. The airforce. Take Iran to pieces, bullets and bombs, just so we know, for sure.
Holly	Where are you?
John	Just so we're safe.

Alice *goes.* **Stephen** *coughs again.* **Mark** *slowly, over the next, turns, kneels and prays.*

Holly	Gran, what are you up to?
Edith	Late night run. Nothing like it, and before you say anything, I'm an old woman, with no money, what's the worse that can happen?
John	And we understand. We know what our leaders are telling us. But my question is – how do you feel?

Amir *and* **Rachel** *are at home.*

Amir	When you say end it? You mean . . .
Rachel	I don't know, it's just nothing works, anymore. Does it?
John	Nervous?
Holly	Gran? . . .
John	Sick?
Holly	Are you okay? . . .

Edith   I'm sorry love, I was just feeling a bit . . .
                     Oh.

Holly   Gran?

Edith *sees something in the ground. Goes over to it.*

John   Alone?

Edith *digs around, pulls on the object. It comes out of the ground –
a child's hand.*

Stephen *collapses.* **Sarah** *shuts her eyes.* **Edith**, *shocked, shuts her
eyes.* **Mark** *praying. Shuts his eyes.* **Holly** *shuts her eyes and prays.*
Shannon, **Zia**, **Rachel** *and* **Amir**, *the same.*

John   Me too.

Of all of them, only **Ruth** *stands – centre stage, her eyes closed.*

                     So. We have to act. Together. This is the
                     moment.

                     We'll meet and march, and we'll take a
                     message to parliament that says we do
                     not want this war. A message that says
                     everything has to change.

                     This is the moment we get better.

                     This is the moment it happens.

                     Yes.

                     In. Our. Name.

Interval

Act Four

One

Trafalgar Square. A protest is raging. A van has been converted into a makeshift stage with a screen. Loud music. Crowds surging. Banners, chanting. Energy and conviction – passion. But good-natured.

In the daylight, **John** *climbs up and stands on the stage, and the music fades.*

John Men and women of Britain! It's a bright day, it's a passionate day and it's time to throw things away and start again. From this day forward we will no longer simply be a country of failure, of guilt and insecurity. Instead, we will be a nation of principle, strength and peace. We will have standards. We will demand things that we have been told are out of date, things like kindness, politeness, welfare, equality. Things like *society*. And in contrast to what our generation has been told since we were born, we don't think it is foolish to believe rather than doubt, we don't think ideology is dead, we don't think it's all about compromise and pragmatism because like the best of men and women before us, we will aspire and yes, we will dream! There can be no progress without belief. Belief in the capacity of mankind, belief that we can be better, that we can be more than animals, more than selfish, more than war-like tribes, pushing each other out the way in brutal competition. The older generation, as they always do, tell us we are naive,

trust us they say, we *know* that change
is impossible. Well they always say that
and it is up to us, with youth and hope
and vision, to show them they are so, so
wrong.

We have an idea. We have a way forward
for this country. And today is our first test.
Today we have been moved to action. We
stand here, every one us committed to the
idea that there is a future for Iran without
innocent men, women and children dying
in their thousands. We believe that with
modern technology and old-fashioned
solidarity, we can empower the Iranians to
follow the example of other young people
across the world, throw off their rulers
and seize their country for themselves.
Our generation is speaking with a clear
voice, stating that one does not need
violence to change the world, one needs
passion, communication and conviction.

Today we say to the government that
storming in with troops and taking over a
country is not how we do things anymore.
Instead, in our names, in this time, we can
communicate to people in every home
in every place. In our name, in this time,
we can reach out and empower them, not
batter and destroy them, in our name we
can demand freedom for Iran, we can
encourage and support them to have a say
over their future – in our name, we can all
be better.

In our name!

Crowd   In our name! In our name! In our name!

John *walks into the crowd, as the chanting continues.*

Two

In Number 10. The protest on television. **Ruth** *and* **Stephen** *are watching it.*

They can also hear it outside.

'In our name!'
'In our name!'

Ruth   One year, we spent Christmas together. I'd already heard about him from Simon. This amazing best friend. He didn't have anywhere to go so Simon invited him back to ours. He arrived with a few clothes, a case of wine and a pile of books. We got on immediately, he spoke like someone much older. We talked into the night, they went for walks.

It was always about the two of them. Him and Simon. They were so . . . bright.

What does he want?

Stephen   He's got something to prove.

Ruth   Maybe. But what if it's worse.

What if he means it?

Three

In the crowd. **Holly**'s *handing out leaflets.* **Mark** *with her.*

Mark   Well I didn't see *this* coming. When I was a student we went to Trafalgar square and got pissed, we just wanted a bottle of Diamond White that's as far as our ambition went, but you lot, you say let's go to the square for a party, you get what? Half a million?

Holly   I don't have time for this.

Mark	You said I was scary.
Holly	You are.
Mark	I'm helping your grandmother, for free. She doesn't think I'm scary when I get her off vandalism charges. I never made you do anything. Scary? What? Now? Am I *scary* now?
Holly	Yes.
Mark	We agreed it was a win–win situation, you were very empowered about it, but now you're saying that every time it happened and every time I paid you, you were in fact –
Holly	Stop –
Mark	Putting up with it.
Holly	Yes.
Mark	But you see *that* –
Holly	Mark –
Mark	That's a different thing – 'putting up with it' – that was *not* what we agreed. You need to be careful.
Holly	*Careful*?
Mark	Of when you say things, what you imply.
Holly	Now you're threatening me.
Mark	*No*!

He's in public. People start to look.

	It's not threatening, I don't mean you need to be careful because I'll hit you –
Holly	Jesus Mark –

Mark	I mean you need to be *careful* of what you imply because when you say something like that to someone – like they're scary – it can go round their head, it has an effect –
Holly	Mark you're a bastard. You say it yourself.
Mark	Fine, but that doesn't mean I'm into *rape* or anything –
Holly	I'm not saying rape.
Mark	– what you're implying –
Holly	I'm not saying that but paying girls for sex is –
Mark	It's a deal.
Holly	Jesus, a *deal*? Okay.
Mark	No, no, don't do that, it is, it's a deal that we *agreed*, that you instigated in the first place – fuck's sake half the women of the world are saying you should take them seriously the other half are telling us don't listen to a word we say, 'when we *say* we're fine with it Mark, we're *obviously* not telling the truth, instead of taking us seriously you should take care of us, as women, and not believe a fucking word'. No definitely means no, but yes does not in any way apparently mean yes. Do women have a right to do what they want with their bodies?
Holly	You know it's wrong but you do it anyway.
Mark	The thing is, the simple thing is Holly, that you've fucked this up, this bit of your life, and you feel bad about it and that's fine, but – you – you – You have to take some *fucking* responsibility for *something*!

She looks at him. Properly. For the first time.

Holly	Men.
Mark	No.

A moment.

Mark	Anyway. I didn't come here for you.
Holly	Why then?
Mark	I can't sleep.
	Where is he?

Four

Number 10. **Martin**, **Liam** *and* **Carol** *are there with* **Ruth** *and* **Stephen**.

Ruth	It's a phone call from Carol. Just testing the water.
Stephen	Why do it at all?
Ruth	The crowd's growing. Support in every city. Blanket television coverage. I have to do something.
Stephen	The people elected you, they want you to be decisive. Get the police out. You've done it before.
Ruth	They're not aggressive, they're not violent.
Stephen	Not yet.
Ruth	There's no harm in listening.
Stephen	By listening, by looking – by acknowledging his existence in any way you give him power.

He coughs. **Martin** *receives a notification on his iPad.*

Martin	Prime Minister

Ruth	What is it?
Martin	It's about Dennis. They're charging his wife.
Ruth	His – oh – God –
Martin	Apparently they're not looking for anyone else.
Ruth	How old was his daughter?
Martin	Eleven.

A moment.

Ruth	What was her name?

No one says anything.

	Martin. Her name?
Martin	I just told you.
Ruth	What?
Martin	I just said Prime Minister.
	Ruby.
	Her name was Ruby.
Ruth	Oh.
Stephen	Are you alright?
Ruth	Martin. Send a message to Dennis. Anything I can do.
Liam	I would advise that you stay very distant from the whole –
Ruth	Send the message. Keep me updated. Carol. Any word back?
Carol	Back?
Ruth	From the square.
Carol	Well. No. It may take some time.

| **Ruth** | Why? |
| **Carol** | These are young people Prime Minister. Easily distracted. |

Five

In the square, **John**, **Rachel**, **Amir**, **Holly**, **Zia** *and* **Shannon** *discuss the call.* **Mark** *stands towards the back, waiting.*

John	Rachel, tell them I want to talk, just me and her, for an hour, this afternoon.
Amir	Why just the two of you?
Zia	We can come as well yeah?
John	No. Thank you.
Zia	But we've got this far –
Rachel	John if she saw how many of us there are –
Shannon	I'd tell her a thing or two –
John	She's watching the television. We've shown our numbers. But now the two of us have to sit and down and talk, listen, face to face. If we do that, we can get what we all want.
	So.
	Alright to make the call Rachel?
Rachel	Okay.
John	Thank you.

Rachel *goes to call.*

Amir	What are you going to talk about?
John	What do you think?
Amir	Simon?
John	Why now?

Amir	What?
John	You hardly talk about it, I've been back for weeks and he's never mentioned, not really, not until now.
Amir	Because you're seeing her for the first time so I thought –
John	You miss him.
Amir	
John	So do I but these people are here for a reason. We're not going to talk about Simon, we're going to talk about a change of direction. Offering something new.
Amir	But she might want to –
John	Amir you wanted me to support the war, then when I disagree and we occupy the square, you change your mind, you stay with us. Why? What persuaded you?
Amir	You.
John	Well then. Trust me.

They look at each other.

Mark *steps forward.*

Mark	Sorry . . . don't want to intrude . . .
John	Mark.
Mark	You remember my name. Good. So the thing is every night I have this dream. The same one they all get. I'm not sleeping, I'm not working, in fact I'm not doing anything at the moment, and the more I thought about it the more strange it was that you knew, back then remember, you looked at me and you could tell.

John	Yes.
Mark	So, anyway, my whole life is, basically, fucked, I'm not just talking about this month, this year, I'm talking about not speaking to my dad because of an argument and then him dying, I'm talking about the love of my life who I cheated on, and now she's gone away, I'm talking about jeopardising a promising career by turning up smelling of booze, and then – she – Holly – said I was *scary* and I've been thinking and maybe, yes, maybe I am – and then these dreams, and in the state I was in, a week ago, I prayed. I fucking. I've never prayed in my life, but I was a mess, so I knelt down and asked for help. I don't know why but I asked for . . . forgiveness, and someone answered.
	And it was you. Your voice.
	Isn't that *weird*?
	So.
	I need to know. Yes? What's going on? Cos I'm like . . . this far . . . from hitting the fan, from the fucking *edge*. Of what I can. Do. So you need to tell me, quickly, really – You need to tell me now.
John	It's okay.
Mark	What?
John	It's okay.
Mark	'Okay.' What the fuck does that . . . it's not, thanks for the words of. *What*?
	Thanks for the –

John *looks at him.* **Mark** *starts crying. He can't help himself.*

Mark	Shit . . . oh . . . fuck . . .

He falls to the floor, **John** *catches him. Holds onto him.*

John	It's alright. It's alright.

Rachel *comes back in.*

John	What did they say?
Rachel	Yes. They said yes.

Six

Number 10. **Ruth**, *with* **Martin**, **Liam** *and* **Carol**.

Ruth	He's not bringing anyone else? None of his followers?
Carol	No.
Liam	The press are calling them his 'disciples'.
Ruth	So that makes him. . .
Liam	Apparently he also does miracles.
Ruth	What miracles?
Martin	He knows when it's going to rain.
Ruth	That's not a miracle Martin, that's the weather forecast –
Carol	Prime Minister. It's important for us all to convey that we think this meeting is a very bad idea, and whatever happens as a result of this meeting we can not take responsibility for it. None of us. Your political advisors, communications –
Ruth	Nothing like support.
Carol	And the civil service.
Ruth	Really *nothing* like support

Liam	If you come out of the meeting giving something away you lose credibility. On the other hand if you don't, people will say you are arrogant and patronising.
Ruth	I understand, I'm on my own. Can you make sure Stephen's here?
Carol	Is he still –
Ruth	Yes. He's still in Number 10. He needed to lie down.
Carol	Where?
Ruth	I don't know.
Carol	Prime Minister –
Ruth	Carol
Carol	You've invited a young man with no credentials except his ability to cause civil unrest into the heart of Number 10, somewhere around the building but we're not sure where is a highly controversial sleeping atheist, outside the window half a million people are protesting in the streets, and the Leader of the Free World might call at any moment to see if we want to go to war.
Ruth	That's right.
Carol	Clear the room please!

They leave. **Martin** *hangs back.*

Liam	She said clear.
Martin	I just . . .
Ruth	What is it?

Liam *goes.*

Martin	If you want to know what the people think, of him, of you . . .

His gives her his iPad.

Martin	Tweets, the news, updating all the time. In case it's useful.
	Prime Minister . . . I think you're right.
	To listen to him. I've been out there – heard him speak –
Ruth	You've not been sleeping have you Martin?
Martin	I don't mean this politically, but over the last year. It feels like it's all falling apart. In the country. Across the world. Like people have gone wrong. And I . . . I think out of everything, he's . . .
	I think he's good.

Seven

A prison cell. **Dennis** *enters.* **Sarah** *is sat.*

Dennis	You know what I want to do? I mean there's people out there who would stop me doing this but I want to tear you to fucking pieces you know that? I want to rip you to shreds to do to you what you did to her, I told them you were protesting your innocence that's the only reason they let me see you, I told them this was a diplomatic matter that's why they let me in, but they'll find out in a few minutes you're guilty as hell.

Sarah *stares at him.*

Dennis	Why? That's what I want to know. I'll never see you again I never want to, I wish they would kill you in this country, I don't care what happens to you. But I want to know why.

Beat.

	They found her in pieces. Cut up with a knife.

Beat.

Sarah	You believe in God.
Dennis	Yes I do.
Sarah	I know you believe there are good things and evil things in this world. I know you believe that.
Dennis	Good things and evil things.
Sarah	Good people and evil people.
Dennis	Yes.
Sarah	And what would you do if you found out there was an evil person in your house if there was an evil person in the world that you had created, people say it about Hitler what would his parents do if they had known, well I knew, I knew what she was going to grow up to be, there was nothing good about her. This is better, I may have taken a life Dennis, but I've saved more. I've saved so many people from the things she would do.
Dennis	You don't have any idea what she –
Sarah	But what if I did. What if I could?
Dennis	You can't.
Sarah	But if I could –

Dennis	You DON'T
Sarah	. . .

She breaks down.

Dennis. I just want you to reach out
and touch me, to say that although you
may hate me and I might be the most
loathsome creature that ever walked,
that you still see me as a human being,
as someone who deserves at least, at least
some compassion.

Dennis   I should be working. I should be in there
– they're going to invade and I was a voice
holding them back but now I have no
influence and we will go to this wrong war,
and many people will die and it won't be
because of Ruby it will be because of you.
You're the evil one.

Sarah   Please. Touch me then you can go.

He stands.

There was a reason.

There was a reason I did it.

She looks at him. Crying now.

Eight

Edith *plays piano as the scene gathers. She watches on the
computer.*

We see everyone outside waiting, hoping.

Number 10. From two different doors enter **Stephen** *and* **John**.

Ruth   John.

She holds out her hand. **John** *sees* **Stephen**.

John   We said it was just going to be us.

Ruth	I thought you wouldn't mind if Stephen joined us for a while.
	We all know each other and it's been such a long time, I'd prefer to have him with us.
John	Stephen. Are you alright?
Stephen	I'm fine,
John	You're ill.
Stephen	A little.
John	Cancer.
Stephen	What?
John	Is it cancer?
Stephen	Well they haven't completed the tests yet, but we're not here to play doctors.

Beat.

Ruth	Shall we sit? They've given us coffee, tea.
John	Tea.
Ruth	No milk is it? Stephen?
Stephen	Coffee.
Ruth	Coffee. Lovely. Coffee for me. So.

The tea and coffee is handed out.

Ruth *sits down. A moment of looking at each other.*

	Where did you go?
John	Away.
Ruth	Away?
John	Yes.
Ruth	Where?

John

Ruth   Everyone thought you were dead.

John   I know.

Ruth   There were people who cared about you.

John   Not that many. I don't have any family.

Ruth   What about your friends.

John   I'm not here to talk about Simon.

Ruth   Alright let's talk about you instead. Where did you go?

A pause.

Ruth   John it's okay. We've got time. I just wanted to know where you'd been. I don't see why it's a secret. I want to get a sense of who I'm talking to.

John   You know me Ruth. I'm the same person, I've gone away, I've grown up, I've worked a few things out but other than that I'm exactly the same. But what about you? When you were younger we thought you were amazing, you were the radical in your party, a Tory but campaigning for all the right things – higher taxes for those that could afford it, social improvement, closing tax loopholes, forcing the banks and the corporations to pay their fair share, we hated your party but we loved you –

Ruth   I know.

John   – but you've been in power two years and what have you done?

Ruth   It's not as simple as / you might think.

John	I'm not saying it's simple, I know it's difficult. It's hard work even when you try but I've studied everything you've done and it's compromise. The easy route. Again and again. Why? And I think that's what this is today.
Ruth	You think war is the easy route?
John	There's another way.
Stephen	She's doing her best.
Ruth	Stephen –
John	She's old enough to speak for herself Stephen.
Stephen	You're right, she's old enough, she's an adult, she takes responsibility, she doesn't have the privilege of going off on some extended gap year and then coming back and just *complaining* she has to balance interests she has to find ways of maintaining the economy while also attempting to reduce the gap between rich and poor and all at the same time taking the short-termist increasingly fickle and small minded electorate with her. It's not as simple as coming in here with a to-do list.
John	It's even in the way she speaks. She's lost something.

He looks at **Ruth**.

John	Why can't we pay more tax?
Ruth	People don't want to.
John	Make the case.
Ruth	It's been proven.

John	It's not been proven. Make the case.
Stephen	Oh come on John.
Ruth	It's been proven that if you increase taxes – if you go to the electorate with that, you'll lose –
John	That's not proof.
Ruth	It's what's happened.
John	It's what's happened recently yes but that's different to proof, just because recent leaders haven't managed to persuade the people why have you given up?
Ruth	Oh John you're so vague it's endearing –
John	If I'm a parent and I want my child to be able to go to university without feeling like they'll live their whole life in debt, if I want decent education for every child in the country, if I feel uncomfortable with the NHS falling into largely private hands, who can I vote for, where is my candidate?
Ruth	John.
John	Where's the politicians who question the idea of choice? You're in pain, you need an operation as soon as possible, you don't want to go *shopping*, it's not your job to choose the right person – you don't want choice you want delivery. Where are the politicians demanding all this? Where's the politicians with new ideas? Again and again, less and less, because we're not *naive* anymore, because this is the only way that works.

	Where are the ideas Ruth, where are the dreams? We should be electing leaders, not managers.
Ruth	John – there's something else we should talk about.
John	You asked me where I've been. This is where I've been. This is what I want. Where's the politician who does all that?
Ruth	John –
John	You Ruth. That's who you were, that's what you used to be like, when we sat up till two on New Year's Eve and we had drunk too much whiskey and ginger, and you used to smoke a bit back then too, and you told me, you said you had *nothing to lose* – you weren't one of the boys you were going to shake things up. Well start today. Take the difficult route. Don't go to war.
Ruth	Sometimes things don't work out as you planned.
John	I know.
Ruth	– things we don't intend.
John	Of course.
Ruth	And sometimes life just gets in the way. Do you understand?
John	*I don't want to talk about Simon.*
Ruth	I didn't mention *Simon.*
Beat.	
John	Ruth . . . It's not too late to actually *do* something people will remember. Something that will change a generation.

Stephen	It is John.
John	No –
Stephen	It is too late. You think you're suggesting something new? Almost of all of what you're saying is impossible. Higher taxes stifle economic growth that is just a fact, and the twentieth century has proved conclusively, and yes it is proof, that the introduction of a free-market capitalism into a country's system not only raises the quality of people's life, but also intrinsically leads to greater social and political freedom.
John	For the rich.
Stephen	At first, but eventually for all.
John	A big eventually, they're still waiting in Russia, South Africa, you could argue we're still waiting here. The chances of rising up the ladder in this country have sharply declined in the last thirty years, you know why –
Stephen	Yes, yes –
John	The free market, smaller government, / less welfare, opportunity –
Stephen	I could debate that, there's increasing population, decreasing resources. But I thought you were here to talk about Iran?
John	I'm here to talk to Ruth.
Stephen	Ruth's listening aren't you?
Ruth	Yes.
Stephen	She's fascinated by us.
Ruth	I like the perspective.

Stephen	Exactly. Now, John – Iran's nuclear intention is something else completely. You criticise us for saying you're naive, well that's difficult because all you out there, you sound it. You sound like *children*. Your criticism is that this *feels* wrong, well of course it does, it's *war*, people are going to die, war always *feels* wrong, it should feel wrong, but the world is nasty and the civilisation you live in, every single tiny aspect of the western civilization is built upon the progress and protection that came at the cost of blood, that your ancestors fought for, even though it felt just as *wrong* then. No one wants this to happen, but we have to protect our interests and we have to be intelligent enough and proud enough to say we think our values are better than theirs – our values of freedom, democracy, equality.
John	I'd question whether equality is currently / one of our values.
Stephen	And we have to be strong enough to know that those things are not givens. Good does not always win out, not under the ancient monarchies, not under Stalin, or Hitler. There's no God, no divine justice. We do not inevitability get better, unless we work, unless sometimes we *fight*.

He's unsteady, sweating, overwhelmed.

Ruth	Stephen –
Stephen	I'm fine. Come on! Let's say it, let's come out and proclaim it loud, our ways are better, yes, *better* than theirs.

John	Whose?
Stephen	The Iranian –
John	The Iranians'?
Stephen	The Iranian regime's. Our systems of power and law and the values we have enshrined are morally superior. We don't make our women hide themselves, we don't beat our children, we don't stone adulterers, homosexuality is legal, we give everyone the vote. We're happy to co-exist and agree to differ but not where our moral principles and the bedrock of our culture are at stake. We cannot allow men we wouldn't trust with our sister to have access to a nuclear weapon.
John	That sounds a bit racist to me.
Stephen	Absolutely not.
John	Who are these men?
Stephen	What?
John	Who do you imagine these men are? Uneducated stupid, Middle Eastern –
Stephen	No, sir, no, quite the opposite, over-privileged well-educated middle-class men, who thrive on corruption and torture, who cultivate a culture of hypocracy and fear, for their selfish desire. There have always been these men. Overgrown children of the world and they should be disciplined, but you'll let them have the bomb.
John	No.
Stephen	Then what's your alternative?

John	It's a different world now Stephen.
Stephen	Really?
John	The world you're describing is the world of the ballot box. Him or her, left or right, valves and switches and binary choices, but to people like me, to us, that way of thinking is ancient. My generation isn't apathetic, we're voting every second of the day – pick up one of these

He grabs the iPad.

Every second every subject, not simply yes or no, this or that, but millions of views, opinions, solutions, the true complexity of the world and all that's needed to pull it together and progress?

Purpose. Conviction, Belief.

He gives the iPad to **Ruth**.

Stephen	How does that stop Iran getting the bomb? You're saying we just sit back and hope –
John	We sit foward. We don't raise a fist. Any government can ultimately not govern without consent. Modern technology has given people more information and more organisation than ever before. It is no longer possible for governments to lie. Therefore, armed with the truth, and the capacity to be heard, it won't be long before the people speak out. We do not need to invade. In Tunisia, Egypt, the people spoke together. And the voice of the people is the –
Stephen	Is the voice of God, and I don't trust either. By all accounts the Muslim

Brotherhood are pretty tech savvy John, and from what I saw out my window earlier this year, riots seem easier to organise than ever – talk about a flash mob –

John   What I'm saying –

Stephen   What are you saying?

John   We have to believe in something.

Stephen   Why?

John   Because the only message at the moment is money, success, power, and it's like a Big Mac, you're told to eat it, but afterwards you're still empty. That's why people are violent and lost and rioting. They've not been given a reason to live. I'm not saying God, but we have to have a motivation towards something, a *drive*. Those people in the square think a thousand different things but today there's something they share. That this is wrong and we can be better. I get emails, letters every day now from people across the country, soldiers, businessmen, old women all after something better. A new idea. They don't want this war. The people of Iran do not want this war.

Stephen   If you allow this technology to get out of control there will be no ideas new or old, everything John, everything will be destroyed. Yes. Armageddon. The end of reality. No light, just darkness. Am I talking your language now? Mystery, apocalypse? I'm told you think dreams have meaning. It's said, coincidence follows you around.

John	Maybe.
Stephen	You said I had cancer. What made you say that?
John	I saw it.
Stephen	Magic?
John	There's things we don't know.

Beat.

Ruth believes in God.

Don't you?

Beat

Ruth	Stephen, maybe John has a point. Perhaps there are other things we could do.
Stephen	Ruth?
Ruth	You've always been a fan of charging in and kicking up a storm.

Beat.

Stephen   If we refuse to take control of this now, our grandchildren will look back and see it as the greatest failure of our generation, far larger than climate change, potentially bigger than the two World Wars. Terrorist nuclear explosions in any place at any time. Imagine that, the constant fear of death, any place, any moment, utterly unavoidable. There would be no freedom at all in that world. True freedom is only ensured through leadership and government. We have a parliamentary democracy for a reason. The people cannot be trusted. Nothing good ever came from literally giving power to the people – civil war, atrocity, mob rule. No. Give power to –

He coughs.

Ruth   Stephen.

Stephen   Give power to –

He coughs again.

Ruth   Stephen go to the hospital.

She picks up the phone.

Hello.

Stephen   Give power to *parliament*. To the experts.

Ruth   I want a car / and a doctor, at the back door, now.

Stephen   The people are stupid and the people are dangerous. They can shout as loud as they want. But –

Martin *enters.*

Ruth   Martin will you show Stephen out?

Martin   Of course.

Stephen *coughs, then looks at her.*

Stephen   Keep your head. Don't be drawn.

It's an act.

Ruth   Thank you.

Stephen *looks at them both, then goes.*

Ruth   What is it?

John   Lung cancer.

Ruth   You're guessing, right?

The phone goes.

Ruth *answers it.*

Ruth	Yes?

She listens.

Yes.

Yes.

Alright.

She hangs up.

Ruth	More tea?
John	No.

Beat.

They look at each other.

Ruth	So I had a kind of breakdown.

You didn't ask so I thought I should tell you, when he died, everything in my life changed as I suppose you would expect, I stopped work, I started just looking into the distance, blanking out. I thought he'd come through the door any second, and reveal it had all been a horrible mistake but no he was gone forever and I knew there had to be a reason. But you told them it was an accident.

John	I'm not here to talk about Simon.
Ruth	This is about Simon of course it is, of *course* it is, don't you *dare* tell me that you would be out there if it wasn't for him! You're pretending, pretending you don't have a past and that it doesn't matter. But you can't run away from this. He was so much *better* than you – you talk about belief? He had real belief he had belief in people. What happened?

John	Ruth –
Ruth	What happened that night John? – you ran away.
John	I had to leave.
Ruth	You felt guilty.
John	There was nothing here for me.
Ruth	You never even spoke to me about it.
John	You want me to tell you.
Ruth	Yes of course.

A tiny beat.

John	There was drink, there was smoking.
Ruth	He didn't smoke.
John	He did.
Ruth	You gave them to him.
John	That night yes, but he did smoke. There was drink, there was weed, we were out Ruth and that's what students do. We were standing on the stone bridge and he said he thought he should jump in. What would it be like?
Ruth	He wouldn't have done that, he wouldn't have suggested it. It was you. That's exactly the sort of thing you would say.
John	No. It was his idea.
	But I didn't stop him. I could've done. I could've stopped him, but I didn't you're right I thought it would be funny, so I stood back and watched and he was there on the bridge and he jumped in just like they do on May Day in the morning just

like we've all seen lots of them do before,
but it was dark and he hit something and
there was a scream and I didn't see him
after that.

You know what happened after that.

It happened in seconds. He was washed
down the river.

Ruth   You've never said sorry.

John   It wasn't my fault.

Beat.

Ruth   What are you doing?

Beat.

John   He would've stopped you.

Ruth   Don't be ridiculous. You don't know what
he would've done.

John   I'm not him. I'm nothing like him I agree,
but he should've been here, he would've
talked to you, you're right I don't know
why it happened. I don't see a plan in
it. But I imagine a universe right now
where he's still alive. I imagine dying and
finding that all this was a computer game,
a fantasy, a projection and he's still there. I
think, bearing in mind how little we know,
that there are possibilities.

But if he is gone forever, that means every
young man in the Iranian army you kill
is gone forever, that means every piece of
collateral damage, every woman, every
child, is gone forever. This has to stop.
He would've told you that. This isn't just
about *feeling* this is about the very nature

of who we are, the kind of actions that make life worth living. What you're doing is empire, it's territory. I think you know you're making a mistake, and Simon would know it too.

Ruth *tries to pour a glass of water but she can't –*

Ruth   You didn't see the baby, the child, you didn't see him grow, he never did *anything* like that until he met you! And now this – you come here? What will you do if I say yes? If I go to war, what will you tell the people out there?

John   I will tell the country to stop work. I will ask them to think of the people of Iran, and bring peace and I will win, Ruth. But I want to go out there and say that you have listened, and we will not bomb Iran, we will instead put all our efforts together into a completely different approach. A new idea. Something that changes this country for good.

Ruth   You're threatening me.

John   It can't happen.

They look at each other.

Ruth   What did he look like, the last time you saw him?

                Please. I'm his mother.

                This is what I . . . want. You were there.

                You're here now.

                So.

                What was the last you saw of him?

Beat.

John   He stood on the wall on the top of the
                    bridge, and behind him was the night sky.
                    He lifted his arms out to jump, and I then
                    suddenly, I don't know if it was the moon,
                    or whatever but he was lit up, bright, then
                    he fell, there was a noise, then silence.

Ruth   . . .

John   But in that last moment, before he
                    jumped, he was happy.

Ruth *looks at him.*

The phone rings.

She picks it up.

Ruth   Yes?

She picks up her iPad. Looks at it.

                    Alright. Yes.

                    Thank you.

She hangs up. Puts the iPad down.

Ruth   Alright.

                    You know what I believe in John? The
                    grey area. The bit between. To any
                    difficult problem, there is never a *right*
                    solution, there is only ever the *best*
                    solution. Nothing on Earth is completely
                    pure. I prefer complexity, difficulty,
                    balance. Good and evil? No. Children's
                    words.

Beat.

                    So this decision, when it's made, it will not
                    ever be completely right, or wrong, it will
                    instead be a matter of judgement.

Beat.

I'm the most popular Conservative leader of this country for decades which you might say is hardly an achievement, but I'm going try to explain something I think you never understood. Why would a nice person like me be a Tory? Why on earth am I not on the left, like a normal compassionate human being? Do I not care? Am I heartless? No. Of course we have to protect the poor, we have to make sure there's equal opportunity, we have to have compassion and *feeling* and *emotion* but it's not those things that have created everything you see around you. Every piece of clothing, every building, every technology, every free democratic principal and institution has been made possible and paid for not by taxes, in the end, but by the market. How did you get that crowd together. Facebook. Twitter. Profit-making companies. It's the most basic function of western civilisation. You go out and you're free to make your way, and if you do well, you're rewarded. That's what makes us happy, and productive and it's my solution to a nasty world. Hard work, opportunity, and in the end, yes, self-interest, looking after your own.

The golden rule.

Look after your own first. Because if you don't do that you can't help anyone. And that's what I intend to do in this case. As the elected representative of this government, it is my first duty to protect the people of this country and allowing Iran to get nuclear weapons is

totally unacceptable. I absolutely believe
in progress, and that's what this will be,
stopping generations of destruction, death
and pain. This isn't about ideology, it's
not about Islam or God or right or left,
it's about complicated, impure *reality* and
protecting the future. Simple as that. In
five minutes, I'll call the President and say
we're in. Tonight, we begin. And that's it.

John   This doesn't make it better. Simon would
                  still –

Ruth   Absolutely. He would disagree completely.
                  But you're right. It isn't anything to do
                  with Simon. This is me. Doing my job.

Beat.

John   You're going to make the call in five
                  minutes.

Ruth   Five minutes yes.

John   Then who was that on the phone?

Ruth   You're not going to start a general strike,
                  you're not going to go out there and do
                  anything. Look.

Ruth *gives him the iPad. As he watches, we see* **Sarah** *on stage in
an interrogation room.*

Sarah   I saw him first at the airport, then later,
                  there he was, outside my house. Why was
                  he outside my house? He said sometimes
                  you have to listen to your instinct
                  even when it doesn't seem right, when
                  everyone is telling you the opposite. He
                  knew what I was struggling with, and he
                  said sometimes you have to do what you
                  believe to be right. He told me to watch
                  him speaking. He knew me. He could *see*.

I did the right thing.

John knows.

I did what was right.

Ruth *switches it off.*

Ruth   She killed her daughter with a knife. Cut her to shreds. Her husband works for the US embassy and while there's absolutely no way legally that footage should be released to the public, he's very keen. He thinks people should know. So I have a feeling it will be out there in about twenty minutes.

John   Ruth, if you believe in what you're doing you don't need to –

Ruth   I'm also going to tell my head of communications to circulate everything about Simon – our involvement, the fact you were there, the personal reason for this protest. It will all come out at five o'clock. To be involved in one death might be a mistake but to be involved in both is too much of a coincidence, even for you.

From outside there begins a faint singing. The crowd outside. Beautiful, choral.

She was eleven. Her name was Ruby. She liked reading and ballet.

John   I had nothing to do with it.

Ruth   I think you make people do stupid things. I think you encourage them to take the brakes off, yes, I think you had something to do with my son's death and I think you had something to do with that little girl's death. You lecture me about compromise, well compromise is safe, compromise is discussion and *thought*. Compromise is experience and making the best possible decision, not the most *exciting*.

This country should have a manager. Look where our leaders took us in the past. It's not about glory and ideologies it's about finding the solution to our problem, and you don't need belief for that you need *graft*.

The singing's louder now. They hear it.

In twenty minutes your friends will find out. They'll see what she has to say and they'll all have the same thought.

They'll realise they've been conned.

And the singing will get quieter.

John   They're stronger than that.

Ruth   The singing will get quieter.

And the singing will stop and become individual voices again. Half a million different opinions. They'll all go back, and get on with their lives.

I have to make a call.

Beat.

John   A lot of people are going to die tonight.

Ruth   I know.

Beat.

John   You had the dream too.

Ruth   What dream?

John   The explosion. The monsters. Every night.

Ruth   Of course. It's all I've been thinking
about. Of course I dreamt of things like
that.

We dream of things that don't exist all the
time.

A long pause. They look at each other.

The singing stops.

Eighteen minutes.

Now. If you'll excuse me. I need to call the
President.

Ruth *goes, leaving* **John** *. . . he turns . . . into . . .*

Nine

Five o'clock – dusk. Trafalgar Square. The sound of the crowd.
Rachel, Amir, Shannon, Zia, Mark *and* **Holly** *wait, fired up.*
The singing changes back to chanting.

'In Our Name!'
'In Our Name!'

John *is led on by two police officers – he looks around. The group
expect him to come to them, but instead he goes to where he made the
speech before.*

It's getting darker now. The crowd sounds fade as they see him.

He steps forward to the microphone.

John   It's two minutes to five.

He pauses.

She listened to everything I had to say.
But . . . she told me she's . . . The bombing
will begin overnight.

There's a silence. He checks his watch again.

13

At five o'clock you're going to receive a message, linking you to a video, and some information. When you watch it, when you read what they have to say, it will make you angry. But before that happens, before you take out your phone and you see what's happened, remember how you feel right now because it's not the object of belief that is important but belief itself. Don't give up. Today we failed, yes, but there will always be failure, and there is so much to do, the terror goes on, the nightmares continue, and men and women and children will die in Iran tonight . . .

. . .

This can happen again, because it's about you, not me, it's all about your conviction and the numbers and the passion and –

It's dark by now. Big Ben chimes. As it does, everyone on stage receives a message – in fact the entire crowd receives a message. And we see them in unison take out their smart phones.

Ten

Thousands of lights illuminating thousands of faces in the dark.

Chaos, shouting, cars being set on fire, violence, rioting and flames.

Fade . . .

The sound of the cello . . . taking us into . . .

Act Five

The cello plays – the twelve stand.

The music finishes and they open their eyes.

Rachel, **Amir**, **Shannon**, **Zia**, **Mark**, **Holly**, **Stephen**, **Ruth**, **Edith**, **Rob**, **Martin**, **Sarah**.

Rachel	We got a cab home. I don't know what happened to him.
Holly	I walked round the streets, my hood up cos otherwise –
Shannon	I went home. Watched it on the TV. The Sky coverage was better cos they had more people out. The BBC was like a phone-in.
Amir	They said Trafalgar Square was like a war zone. I thought bearing in mind what's happening tonight, that's an unfortunate way to put it.
Ruth	For me, that night was strangely quiet.
	Once the order was given, I was updated hour to hour, but the way it works – they just get on with it.
Stephen	In these final weeks of my life, as I face death, I've thought about whether I would have been prepared to die for others, in war? Would I have made that sacrifice? And the answer is yes, absolutely, – to protect the country I love? My way of life? I'm certain. Death is not the worst thing.
Edith	I don't know what's happening to me. Parts of who I am drifting away. I remember something happened recently,

	when I was outside, something in the ground but . . . You see the thing is I can't even practise the piano properly, because I can't remember what I've already learnt. I could just be playing the same tune over and over again. The world's a bitch. And that man . . .
Mark	I got a cab, couldn't face going back to my flat, so instead, weirdly I went *home*.
Edith	Best to put an end to it. I've ordered the pills on the internet and it seems quite straightforward. I don't want anyone to worry.
Ruth	History will judge, that's what I'm saying, in interviews, again and again. But it won't. Was it worth the loss of life? Is the world better now?
Edith	The strange thing is, I've believed in heaven my whole life. But now I'm facing it, and with the dreams. Well
Ruth	I don't know.
Edith	I'm not so sure.
Beat.	
Zia	It took me two days to call her, I was scared cos she's not my usual type I mean I normally go for the pretty ones not that this girl isn't pretty but she doesn't get bored of me which is good she's interested so that's we do Stephen Hawking impressions together? So that's . . . I mean . . . Yeah.
Holly	He can't have gone up to Trafalgar, people would have seen him. The same if he'd

gone towards Green Park, so he must've
gone down Whitehall, but even then.
Maybe he got a cab or something – I called
the firms but – that night was –

Mark   I'm gutted any of it had anything to do
with him, but yeah . . .

Holly   I'll keep looking.

Mark   Mum was surprised to see me –

Holly   I'll wait –

Mark   – she cleared out the old room, didn't ask
too many questions, thank god, just told
me about her garden. She's growing peas,
apparently.

Zia   Her name's Shannon.

Shannon   I'm starting this course. Zia's idea.

Zia (*Stephen Hawking impression*) Shannon! Huh! – She's
doing this course now.

Shannon   Open University. Physics. It's good. And
you get free pens.

Beat.

Sarah   Here, my life is simple.

I'm on my own, for protection, because
all the others, they know what I did. It's
simple. I wake, dress, pray, read . . .

Martin   I quit. Got myself off Twitter, cleared my
Facebook account.

Sarah   Of course I think of her all the time.

Martin   Thing was, whenever the Prime Minister
talked about the tactics, I saw this look on
her face. I don't think she was ever . . .
certain. I'm going to be a teacher. I want

a small life. Don't think there's anything much anyone can do, except get through it.

| **Amir** | We both still wake in the night, facing each other. |

| **Ruth** | At night, I think of Simon, of course. |

| **Rachel** | We've talked about a baby but – |

| **Ruth** | What would he say? |

| **Mark** | I found this old video of me as a kid. I've got this stick and I'm digging a hole in the back garden. Dad's filming it. But anyway I watched it and I thought how did he, this kid, smiling, mucking about with a stick . . . how did he . . . become . . . this . . . |

| **Amir** | If we have a kid, he could have the dreams too. |

| **Mark** | What happened? |

| **Amir** | And we wouldn't know. Cos, well, kids scream anyway. |

| **Sarah** | No. I don't sleep well. How could I? |

| **Ruth** | Sometimes at night, I pick up the phone and go to call someone. |

| **Shannon** | It's on the news every night. |

| **Ruth** | I always hang up in the end. Go back to bed. |

| **Shannon** | Every time I see it, the war, I think was there something we could've done? Something better – |

| **Amir** | It's different when you know people out there, who are in the houses, with the |

	lights out at night, hiding under the table. I don't know what I was thinking.
Shannon	And the dreams –
Amir	It was wrong. Of course. Rachel's still out every day, campaigning.
Rachel	Problem is you start to think what it's all going to look like, in twenty years? How does this ever stop? We need something . . .
Ruth	I lie awake, scared of what I'll see when I close my eyes. Dennis was right.
Shannon	I think the dreams are something to do with –
Ruth	I do need someone. I do.

Beat

Rob   I thought I'd know. And I thought he'd help. Cos I'd worked out it was going to be important to know and that's what got me listening to him in the first place. I thought he'd help me especially with these fucking dreams. I thought it was nerves. Going out there for the first time. Made sense.

So I followed him on the TV. On the internet. The protest. The speeches. The riot. And then . . .

Then obviously. Decision made. We were sent in. And. It was. Well. What you saw.

And then pretty soon, we're in charge, security you know, all lessons learned from Iraq, while they're training the police force up, sorting out the interim

government and I'm on this road block,
and I'll tell you I've got this far and I
haven't had to actually shoot at anyone.
Covering fire but not actually at, anyone,
and I'm on this road block and suddenly
there's this woman and she's coming
towards me, and she's wearing this
massive fucking black thing, and her eyes
are – are – anyway I'm under orders to
not let anyone near this cos they might
be you know suicide bombers all that, so
I shout to her stay back, and she's a good
way off but she's still coming towards me.
She's running now and I've got the gun
up and I'm gesturing and shouting, like
get back but she's coming towards me
faster and faster and by now I can see
her eyes, and this is the moment yeah
I thought this is what the dreams are
about and everything that he was saying.
Cos I'm looking at her eyes, in fact that's
pretty much all I can fucking see – her
eyes, and I can't tell . . . and I can't tell if
her eyes are scared, and she's running
away, towards us, for help and she's good,
maybe she's a mother with children and
these are just the eyes of a loving woman.
Or if no – they're angry and she's running
at us, to kill us and she's well trained and
she's fucking . . . evil. I . . . I don't know.
But I've got to make a decision *now* and
the training is just fucking do it, and I'm
doing all what you're supposed to but in
the end we can't risk it so I open fire and
shoot her across the chest and one goes in
her head and she's down, quickly. Lots of
blood.

You know what's . . . what I can't deal with?

I still don't know.

Turned out she didn't have a bomb. She did have a knife, but they didn't know if that was self-defence, or to do some proper damage.

So in the end we can't tell. If she was good, or evil.

Why she was running.

And that was it. That's what I wanted to know. From him.

I'm ready to fight. To protect the people I love. My way of life.

But I needed to know what the enemy looked like.

But . . . now he's gone.

And he's just . . .

Left us all to – work it out for ourselves.

End

Methuen Drama Modern Plays

include work by

Edward Albee
Jean Anouilh
John Arden
Margaretta D'Arcy
Peter Barnes
Sebastian Barry
Brendan Behan
Dermot Bolger
Edward Bond
Bertolt Brecht
Howard Brenton
Anthony Burgess
Simon Burke
Jim Cartwright
Caryl Churchill
Complicite
Noël Coward
Lucinda Coxon
Sarah Daniels
Nick Darke
Nick Dear
Shelagh Delaney
David Edgar
David Eldridge
Dario Fo
Michael Frayn
John Godber
Paul Godfrey
David Greig
John Guare
Peter Handke
David Harrower
Jonathan Harvey
Iain Heggie
Declan Hughes
Terry Johnson
Sarah Kane
Charlotte Keatley
Barrie Keeffe

Howard Korder
Robert Lepage
Doug Lucie
Martin McDonagh
John McGrath
Terrence McNally
David Mamet
Patrick Marber
Arthur Miller
Mtwa, Ngema & Simon
Tom Murphy
Phyllis Nagy
Peter Nichols
Sean O'Brien
Joseph O'Connor
Joe Orton
Louise Page
Joe Penhall
Luigi Pirandello
Stephen Poliakoff
Franca Rame
Mark Ravenhill
Philip Ridley
Reginald Rose
Willy Russell
Jean-Paul Sartre
Sam Shepard
Wole Soyinka
Simon Stephens
Shelagh Stephenson
Peter Straughan
C. P. Taylor
Theatre Workshop
Sue Townsend
Judy Upton
Timberlake Wertenbaker
Roy Williams
Snoo Wilson
Victoria Wood

Printed in Poland
by Amazon Fulfillment
Poland Sp. z o.o., Wrocław